The Philosophy of Nietzsche:
A Critical Essay

The Philosophy of Nietzsche:
A Critical Essay

Written by
Evgeny Nikolayevich Trubetskoy

Translated by
Filip Poutintsev

Original Russian edition published in 1903:
Философия Ницше. Критический очерк
Евгений Николаевич Трубецкой

ISBN: 978-1-971286-01-3

Publisher: Filip Poutintsev
poutintsev.com
filip@poutintsev.com

Translation and Introduction: Filip Poutintsev

Copyright © 2025 Filip Poutintsev. All rights reserved.

Cover photograph: Friedrich Nietzsche in Basel, Switzerland, c. 1875
Cover design: Filip Poutintsev

Table of Contents

Introduction 6
The Philosophy of Nietzsche: A Critical Essay 9
Chapter: I 13
Chapter: II 17
Chapter: III 24
Chapter: IV 29
Chapter: V 38
Chapter: VI 41
Chapter: VII 47
Chapter: VIII 51
Chapter: IX 57
Chapter: X 63
Chapter: XI 73
Chapter: XII 78
Chapter: XIII 85
Chapter: XIV 90
Chapter: XV 95
Chapter: XVI 102
Chapter: XVII 109
Chapter: XVIII 112
Chapter: XIX 116
Chapter: XX 121
Chapter: XXI 124
Chapter: XXII 127
Chapter: XXIII 130
Chapter: XXIV 134
Chapter: XXV 146
Citations 154

Introduction

All of Nietzsche's philosophy, whose starting point is atheism and whose ultimate result is the negation of man, is an attempt to overcome the fear of death and to answer the question of whether life is worth living at all. The author sets himself the goal of determining how the philosopher coped with this task, and concludes that Nietzsche's doctrine – although in all his works one feels great philosophical and artistic talent, depth in posing questions, subtlety of observation and critique, wealth and brilliance of imagery – bears the stamp of the decline of philosophical thought, while the final conclusions of his philosophy verge on banality. This colossal disproportion between the forces expended and the result achieved is explained by the general weakening and exhaustion of thought, which is a characteristic feature of the modern epoch, in contrast to the days of philosophy's highest flourishing, when it was inspired by faith in reason and in thought as the foundation of existence.

Evgeny Nikolayevich Trubetskoy (1863–1920) was a Russian philosopher of the Tsarist era, a jurist, and a religious and social figure; professor at the Universities of Kyiv (1897–1905) and Moscow (1905–1917). His father was the musicologist Nikolai Petrovich Trubetskoy, one of the founding members of the Moscow Conservatory, and his brother was another famous philosopher of that time, Sergei Nikolaevich Trubetskoy. Their family was an influential noble house formed in the 14th century, descending from the grandson of Gediminas (1275–1341), Grand Duke of Lithuania.

After the Revolution, the Trubetskoy family, along with other noble families, opposed the Bolsheviks and supported the White Army. However, when the Red Army prevailed, most of them, including his son, the philosopher and writer Sergei Evgenievich Trubetskoy, emigrated to France. Evgeny himself did not make it, as he died during the Civil War in 1920 of typhus.

Trubetskoy's book – one of the most complete and detailed works on Nietzsche's philosophy in Russia – occupies a leading place in terms of citations in Russian Nietzsche scholarship of the early twentieth century.

The study is written from religious-liberal positions: the author continues the line of Lopatin–Grot–Solovyov contra Nietzsche. However, in the spirit of his time (by 1903 a pro-Nietzschean literary tradition had already formed and gained strength in Russia), Trubetskoy does not deny the German thinker's philosophical and artistic talent, and even notes several positive aspects of his doctrine: the call to reconsider contemporary cultural and moral values, the protest against the trivialization and degeneration of modern man, the search for the ideal of a rational and moral personality. The guiding motive of Nietzsche's work, Trubetskoy defines as the search for the meaning of life from the standpoint of a consistently developed atheism. It is precisely in atheism, in his deep conviction, that the Nietzschean pathos of contempt for man and culture is rooted.

Trubetskoy sets himself the task of refuting Nietzsche's "attacks" on modern civilization, religious beliefs, philosophical ideas, and the socio-ethical ideals of the age. Practically all the central problems of Nietzsche's philosophy come into focus in his study: metaphysics, epistemology, ethics, religion, social and political questions. The sharpest edge of Trubetskoy's critique is directed against the coexistence of opposing theses in Nietzsche's teaching, calling his work a "labyrinth of contradictions," the chief of which he considers the juxtaposition of philosophical pessimism with an optimistic faith in the meaning of life and in the higher destiny of man.

Trubetskoy structures his analysis on the principle of a triad: first comes an exposition of Nietzsche's views on a given question, then a critique of the position with citations from Nietzsche himself, and finally a conclusion about the artificiality and lifelessness of his judgments.

Trubetskoy's essay is written in clear and understandable language, and since it summarizes well the messages and ideas of Nietzsche's works, it is excellently suited as a first book for someone being introduced to Nietzsche's philosophy. Nevertheless, thanks to Trubetskoy's profound and precise analysis, it is also well suited for the advanced Nietzsche enthusiast as well as for students of philosophy.

Although Friedrich Nietzsche wrote his works about 150 years ago, his message is still relevant. He was ahead of his time and was able to foresee the impact of 20th- and even 21st-century social and political trends. Nietzsche's ideas today remain actual, even more so than during his lifetime, when democratic, socialist, and liberalist ideas were only beginning to develop. For only now do we see the kind of transformation these ideologies truly brought with them.

The Philosophy of Nietzsche: A Critical Essay

"In our time it sometimes happens, – says Nietzsche, – that a man generally gentle, moderate, and restrained suddenly falls into a rage, breaks dishes, overturns a laid table, shouts, rages, insults everyone and everything, and finally withdraws aside, ashamed and angry at himself. For what, why? For starving in solitude, or for suffocating in his own memories? For a man endowed with the needs of a refined, fastidious soul, who rarely finds his table laid and food prepared, the danger is always great; but in our days it is extreme. Cast into the midst of a noisy and vulgar age, with which he is unable to share meals, he may easily perish of hunger and thirst, or else of sudden nausea, if he nevertheless decides to eat from the common dish. In all probability, each of us has had to sit in the wrong place at the common table; and precisely the most gifted among us, those hardest to satisfy, know this dangerous dyspepsia which arises from sudden insight and disappointment in the food or in one's table companions – the after-dinner nausea."[1]

Here Nietzsche describes his own quarrel with the age, his own disappointment and withdrawal from contemporary society. In the feast of modern civilization, everything repels him, both the fellow diners and their spiritual food, both man and his ideals. "There are days, – he says, – when I am visited by a feeling darker than the darkest melancholy – contempt for man. And to dispel any doubts as to whom and what I despise, I will say plainly: I despise the present man, with whom I am fatally bound, as a contemporary. The present man! I suffocate from his foul breath!"[2] This is not about some separate phenomena of modern mankind: Nietzsche's philosophy is a bold challenge to modernity as a whole, a protest against everything that sustains modern man, against his religious beliefs and philosophical ideas, against our ideals, social and ethical, against modern science and art. "My philosophy, – he says, – contains the victorious thought which must destroy every other mode of thought."[3] This is above all a destructive critique which wishes to leave not one stone upon another in the edifice of modern culture.

In his negative relation to reality, Nietzsche does not confine himself to modernity alone. Declaring himself in all respects an "untimely man," he shows relative tolerance toward past times, but even this tolerance costs him an effort: for him, human history is a history of mental diseases, and historical studies themselves he compares to wandering in a madhouse.[4] As the fruit of all previous human development, our age contains elements of the Middle Ages and antiquity, fragments of all preceding cultures. Therefore, Nietzsche's all-around denial of modernity turns into a denial of man and of mankind in general. Among men, he finds no one who would justify the existence of man and our faith in him.[5]

And not only is man the object of his denial. Man is a partial phenomenon of the universe, consequently a partial manifestation of that general disorder, that general absurdity which our philosopher perceives in all existence. Therefore, for Nietzsche, it is not enough to "overcome man",[6] he sees the task of his thought in "overcoming the universe".[7]

This negation does not exhaust Nietzsche's philosophy: negation is only one side, one tendency of his thought. To deny reality is possible only from the standpoint of some positive ideal opposed to existence as something desirable, obligatory. "When we deny, – says Nietzsche, – this means that within us there is something that wants to live and affirm itself, something that perhaps we do not yet see and do not yet know."[8] Overthrowing the "idols" of modern mankind and "destroying its sanctuaries," the philosopher wants to "erect a new shrine" on their ruins.⁹ His philosophical task he himself defines as the "revaluation of all values": it comes down to replacing everything hitherto considered good and valuable with new "true" values.

Nietzsche's philosophy, as is clear from this, is an attempt to settle accounts with the whole past and present of mankind. This attempt, in any case, deserves serious attention. If Nietzsche succeeded in stirring his age, if today his name is on the lips of every educated person, this is conditioned not by a whimsical or accidental fascination, not by a mere caprice of fashion, but mainly by the seriousness of the questions he raised and the extraordinariness of his gifts.

Nietzsche's doubts and demands have acquired universal interest, and this alone already proves that in them is concealed something more than mere eccentricity. "When a man resists his whole time, blocks its way and demands an account from it, this must have an effect. Whether he wants it or not is indifferent; what matters is that he can do it."¹⁰ In these words, Nietzsche best expresses the significance his philosophy can have for us. He has set forth a series of theses against modern man and modern culture. True or false, these theses in any case cannot remain without influence on us, if only because they compel us to self-examination, to a critical revision of everything that in our time is considered valid and valuable. Even if this revision does not lead us to a "revaluation of all our values," in any case, it will help us separate the wheat from the chaff: spurious, illusory values will not withstand philosophical criticism and will fall away; what in contemporary philosophical thought is truly valuable will obtain for us a deeper and more solid foundation.

A critical evaluation of Nietzsche's teaching can render us another, no less important, service. In this philosophy, with extraordinary force was expressed the dissatisfaction of modern mankind with its present and its painful anxiety for the future. In Nietzscheanism, there found expression the acute crisis of European thought and the foreboding of a danger threatening mankind in the future. "For a long time already, – says Nietzsche, – the development of our European culture has been taking place amid tension and torment, which increase with every decade and seem to approach a catastrophe." At the turn of the two centuries, Nietzsche's philosophy sounds like a dark prophecy. Prophetic personalities, he says, are above all suffering personalities: their gift of foreseeing the future serves them as a source of torment. This thought he immediately explains by a comparison: certain animals suffer strongly from atmospheric electricity. Because of this, some of them, for example, monkeys, possess the ability to foretell a storm. Long before the appearance of clouds, they sense the accumulation of electricity in the surrounding atmosphere and, foreboding a change of weather, behave as though expecting an enemy, preparing for defense or flight. Do we not think that their sufferings are prophetic sufferings.[11]

In Nietzsche's sufferings was expressed the condition of the modern social atmosphere, saturated with electricity. They are of interest to us both as symptoms of a social disease with which modern mankind is infected and as a prophetic phenomenon.

CHAPTER: I

Nietzsche's Worldview in the First Period of His Literary Activity

In Nietzsche's philosophical activity, it is customary to distinguish three periods:[12]

1. The period of fascination with the ideas of Schopenhauer and Wagner;
2. The period of positivism;
3. The properly Nietzschean period (the period of Zarathustrism, in Gast's expression)

Looking more closely at this division, we are convinced that it is somewhat arbitrary and artificial. There is no doubt that the epoch of fascination with the ideas of Schopenhauer and Wagner constitutes a distinct, sharply outlined period of Nietzsche's philosophical development. The transition from Schopenhauer's metaphysics to positivism, i.e., to a principled rejection of all metaphysics, was indeed a fundamental turning point in his worldview. A most superficial comparison of our author's early works with that series of his writings beginning with *Human, All Too Human* (1876–1879) is enough to show that here we are dealing with two fundamentally different and even opposed philosophical doctrines.

On the contrary, between the works of Nietzsche usually assigned to the second and third periods of his philosophical development, there is no such fundamental difference; it is impossible to indicate a philosophical principle that would mark the boundary between these two periods. The negative attitude toward metaphysics is characteristic not only of the middle epoch of Nietzsche's activity, but of all his works written after 1876;

in this sense, he remained a positivist to the end of his days. Therefore, it is hardly correct to speak of some "third period" of his work that supposedly replaced his "positivist" period. Riehl characterizes this third period as a union of positivism with romanticism; here, therefore, the matter is not a change in the basic principles of Nietzsche's teaching, but only a supplementing of his positivism with new elements; new here, apparently, is the cultural-ethical ideal of the "overman," which constitutes the essence of Zarathustra's doctrine. It is easy to see, however, that the novelty of this fundamental dogma of "Zarathustrism" compared with Nietzsche's earlier works lies mainly in its name. Already in *Human, All Too Human* the essential features of our philosopher's "immoralism" are clearly outlined; already here he contemplates the ideal of a personality risen above the opposition of good and evil, "freely and fearlessly soaring above men, morals, laws, and ordinary evaluations of things";[13] here we undoubtedly have to do with the ideal of the "overman," although without this name. Gast admits that the basic principles of Zarathustra's teaching are already contained in Nietzsche's works of the first period, in his *Birth of Tragedy* and *Untimely Meditations*.[14] "Zarathustrism" in general represents nothing more than a further development and elaboration of ideas expressed in earlier works, usually referred to the second or even the first period of Nietzsche's literary activity; hence, it is hardly possible to regard it as some special third period of our author's philosophical creativity.

Among the features distinguishing the second period from the third, researchers usually point to the intellectualism of Nietzsche's second period: in the middle epoch of his activity he saw in life "an experiment of the knower," whereas later he placed the goal of life in the manifestation of the power of personality, in the dominion of its will; in his last works, according to Riehl, he regarded "life for knowledge" as an expression of false asceticism. From this point of view, Nietzsche's return to

Schopenhauer's voluntarism appears characteristic of the third period.

It is easy to see that here, too, we are dealing with imaginary, apparent distinctions. First, the very understanding of life as "the experiment of the knower" is expressed by Nietzsche in his *Gay Science*, i.e., precisely in a work usually assigned to the third period of his activity.[15] Further, the very term "intellectualism" as applied to the middle epoch of our author's activity requires essential reservations; in this epoch, as in the subsequent one, two opposite currents struggled in his thought – faith in reason and denial of reason. Precisely the book *Human, All Too Human*, i.e. the main work of the so-called middle epoch of Nietzsche's activity, is permeated with a skeptical attitude toward reason; here the theme of the illogicality of our whole life, of the incapacity of our reason for knowledge, is extensively developed, in consequence of which, strictly speaking, we ought to refrain from all judgments.[16] In this same book, the impotence of human reason is explained by the fact that it is an instrument of our will, of our passions.[17] Hence, it is evident that here too Nietzsche remains faithful to Schopenhauer's teaching on the primacy of will over intellect; therefore, "voluntarism" does not constitute any distinction between the second and third periods of his work.

The inconsistency of dividing Nietzsche's philosophy into three periods leads, among other things, to certain oddities in the exposition of those researchers who adhere to this division. Thus, for example, Vaihinger assigns the book *Dawn* only "partly" to the second period of our philosopher's development!

On the basis of the foregoing considerations, it seems to me that in Nietzsche's work it is necessary to distinguish not three but only two clearly outlined periods, with the boundary between them being the year 1876, when Nietzsche finally became disillusioned with Schopenhauer and Wagner. It goes without saying, however, that the development of our thinker does not cease after 1876; but it is expressed not in a change of the basic principles of his teaching, but in the supplementing and perfecting of one and the same point of view, to which the philosopher remains faithful to the end of his activity.

CHAPTER: II

The influence of Schopenhauer's philosophy and Wagner's music in the first period of Nietzsche's philosophical-literary activity corresponded to two fundamental inclinations of his mind and heart – his philosophical negation of reality and his striving for the renewal of life through art. From his own confessions, we know what these two influences meant to him. In that time of pessimism, only Wagner's music could make life bearable for him. Therefore, in 1876, when Nietzsche became disillusioned with this music, he felt depressed. The loss was irreplaceable for him; more than ever, he felt the emptiness and aimlessness of his existence.[18]

What Schopenhauer meant to him at that time, we learn mainly from his early works. In the essay *On the Relation of Schopenhauer to German Culture*, written in 1872, he calls the great pessimist the only German philosopher of the nineteenth century: in all German culture, he recognizes as valuable only what Schopenhauer could call his own.[19] The influence Schopenhauer had on him is explained, according to Nietzsche, by three qualities of this philosopher – his honesty, his cheerfulness, and his constancy. He is honest because, unconcerned with outward success, he addresses himself only to himself in his works, writing only for himself; he is cheerful because he has overcome by thought the most significant difficulties; finally, he is constant, because such is his nature.[20]

Schopenhauer sought in philosophy not self-consolation, but truth. In him, love of truth prevailed over base inclinations, over the animal striving for happiness. Having posed the question of the goal and meaning of existence, the philosophical question which Nietzsche rightly regards as central, he did not fear to resolve it in a negative sense and to destroy the illusion of happiness. Therefore, Nietzsche sees in Schopenhauer the highest type of philosopher; he honors in him the heroism of thought unafraid of any conclusions.

The search for the meaning of life was from the beginning Nietzsche's basic aspiration and guiding motive of his philosophizing. Already, the very fact of such a search opens an abyss between the philosopher and other men, condemns him to solitude and seclusion. Among men, he says, it is unusual to ask, "Why do I live, what lesson does life give me, how did I become what I am, and why do I suffer from life?" Everything in life is directed to distract man from this most important task into the realm of everyday, commonplace interests. To the question, "Why do I live?" most people answer without hesitation: "In order to be a good citizen, a scholar, a statesman." In short, the vast majority of men are absorbed in those temporary, passing tasks set before them by their state, family, church, society: all their activity is directed to silencing within themselves the higher consciousness, to forgetting themselves in pursuit of happiness and in blind attachment to life, for the sake of life. They cling with their hearts to the state, to money, to the service of science, or to society only in order not to possess this consciousness; many of them devote themselves to heavy daily labor, in greater measure than is needed to sustain their existence, solely so as not to come to themselves.[21]

Exceptions to this general rule are not even those who, by the nature of their activity, should be bearers of a higher cultural ideal – scholars. The scholars of our day present a strange, paradoxical phenomenon. Their greed in the accumulation of knowledge is boundless; it gives them no rest by day or by night; for them, the pursuit of science is something like factory labor, where the slightest loss of time entails punishment; they are ready to spend a whole lifetime on small, particular research tasks. Meanwhile, it does not occur to them to ask the most important general question: what is the purpose of their labor, their haste, their restless pursuit of knowledge, what is the culture their science is supposed to serve? They miss precisely the most essential questions that arise at every step of scientific research – why, for what, whence![22]

For the philosopher, such self-lulling of consciousness is intolerable. He wants to trace life to its source and its striving. But this means for him to suffer in life. In the becoming world, in the stream of endlessly changing phenomena, everything is empty, deceptive, and flat; everything is worthy of our contempt. The solution of that riddle which the philosopher strives to know lies not in this realm of change and motion, but in being eternal, imperishable, incapable of being otherwise.[23]

In philosophical contemplation, man rises above time; only in such contemplation does life acquire meaning and value. He who ties his existence to some temporary and transitory goal, who wants to be a moment in the development of some human society, state, or science, and wishes thus to belong entirely to the realm of the transient, has not understood the lesson taught by life and must learn it anew.[24]

At this stage of his development, Nietzsche's philosophy manifests itself above all as a search for the unconditional: "Every existence, – he says, – which can be denied, by that very fact deserves to be denied. To be truthful means to believe in such an existence which, in general, cannot be denied, which is itself true and has no falsehood within it."

Therefore, the truthful man realizes the meaning of his activity as a metaphysical meaning, which finds its explanation in the laws of higher life. Here, philosophical contemplation ceases to be negation and turns into affirmation.[25] The true philosopher denies the everyday interests that sustain other men because he affirms the higher goals of human life: he condemns surrounding reality, he takes a negative attitude toward everything that flows in time, because the true meaning of existence for him lies beyond time, in that which endures eternally.[26]

In other words, the philosopher's negative relation to surrounding reality is conditioned by the fact that he stands on a supra-historical point of view: he expects the salvation of man not from process, but from that which lies outside process; for him the world is complete and finished at each given moment of its existence, the past identical with the present; for in all ages of the universe's existence, in the diversity of its phenomena, one and the same eternal, imperishable types are embodied: process cannot create anything new; the world remains always the same in its value and in its meaning.[27]

Such a supra-historical point of view seems alien to the mass of men; it is understandable that in the eyes of the crowd, all the philosopher's activity is sheer destruction, violation of all accepted laws. In reality, however, it is the creation of new conditions of existence worthy of man. The philosopher is faced with a twofold task – theoretical and practical: he must know the universe in its imperishable forms, in its eternal essence; after resolving this theoretical task, he must, with unrestrained courage, work at the improvement of mutable reality.[28]

In other words, the task of the philosopher is to see clearly himself and to bring meaning into what surrounds him, to free himself and others from senseless animal craving. The life of most people is a continuation of animal life. Those who are under the power of the herd instinct and live without awareness of the purpose of their existence have not yet risen above the level of the animal world. "As long as man seeks happiness in life, he has not yet risen above the horizon of the animal; the only difference is that with greater consciousness, he desires what the animal seeks in blind striving." The mass movements of men, their founding of cities and states, their wars, accumulation and squandering of wealth, cries of triumph and pleas for help – all this is the continuation of the animal in man.[29] The goal of true culture lies precisely in replacing this blind striving with the conscious will of the philosopher.[30]

The philosopher embodies the type of true man who has

ceased to be an animal (*Nichtmehr Thier*). He is that higher stage of being toward which history strives, which nature unconsciously seeks in its blind craving. In the pursuit of illusory, vain goals, the animal world suffers without cease. To blunt the sting of suffering, one must be freed from the vanity of animal existence, and for this, one must see clearly, come to clear consciousness. That is why all nature longs for enlightenment; that is why it unconsciously gravitates toward man, seeks to bring forth from itself the type of the true, conscious man. The best representatives of mankind – great artists, philosophers, and saints – illuminate the dark depths of nature with the bright light of consciousness. That is why they embody the secret hope of all creation: their appearance is, as it were, the joyful leap of nature, which has understood itself and attained its goal.[31]

From this are determined the tasks of authentic culture. The meaning of the history of mankind lies not in the contentment of the masses, not in the happiness of all or most of the human race, but in those genial, "supra-historical" individuals who constitute exceptions to the general rule. The goal of history is not to produce the most significant possible number of specimens of the herd-man, the common man, but to bring forth great artists, philosophers, and saints. The goal of mankind's development, as of any animal or plant species, is expressed not in the mass, but in those singular specimens that rise above the general level and therefore signify the transition to a higher type. The masses deserve attention in a threefold way: as blurred copies of great men, printed on poor paper with worn clichés; as a force resisting great men; and, finally, as an instrument of great men. The ordinary man represents only a stage in the universal striving toward the type of the true man: he must regard himself as nature's failed attempt and as testimony to its higher intentions. He must set his goal in contributing to the production of those great personalities who possess the highest human qualities – fullness of knowledge, love, and power.[32] The appearance of a great philosopher on earth has immeasurably greater significance than the existence of this or that university or state,[33] for in him the highest goal is attained – the redemption and humanization of nature.[34]

Such is the general outline of Nietzsche's worldview in the first period of his philosophical creativity. It is easy to see that at its base lies a profound contradiction: two irreconcilable extremes are combined in it – pessimism and an optimistic faith in the meaning of life, in the higher destiny of man. On the one hand, Nietzsche is penetrated by the consciousness of the aimlessness of being, of the senselessness of the world process: "In infinite time and infinite space," he says, "there are no goals".[35] From this point of view, of course, "neither the metaphysical, nor the moral, nor the aesthetic value of existence can be proved".[36] On the other hand, the great man for him is the goal of nature and the goal of mankind's historical development; the production of great men is nature's secret intention. On the one hand, a goal, in Nietzsche's view, is something alien to nature, invented by man, the result of his subjective creativity; on the other hand, the great man is, as it were, the completion of a purposive process of development, the highest stage in the objective realm of ideas.

With this is connected Nietzsche's contradictory evaluation of the significance of the individual: on the one hand, in the basis of individual existence lies apparently no objective goal. "If no one can answer you the question why you exist," says Nietzsche, "then try at last to justify the meaning of your existence, so to speak *a posteriori*, and for this set yourself a task and a goal, some *for what*, an exalted and noble *for what*. Perish for this goal; I know no better life-task than to perish for something great, impossible."[37] Here he is speaking of a purely subjective goal, invented by the individual for his own use. But how can such an understanding of the significance of the individual be reconciled with those passages cited above, where the most outstanding representatives of mankind are spoken of as saviors and redeemers, as embodying the hope of all creation? If our goals are only individual, only subjective, then how can one speak of a common striving, of common hopes, and therefore of common goals of all beings? How, under these conditions, can the appearance of the great man be "the joyful leap of nature, which has attained its goal"? If, finally, the meaning of what exists lies in that which is beyond time, beyond the diversity of individual beings, then how can the efforts of the individual in time be justified? Is it possible to speak even of individual, subjective goals of existence if everything existing in time, everything individual as such, is meaningless?

The contradictory evaluation of the significance of the individual is connected to the contradictory evaluation of the world process. If the world at every given moment of its existence is complete and finished, then the world process in no case is progressive movement: in such a case, the process is not only aimless in its source, but cannot be justified even *a posteriori*; meaning cannot be introduced into that which by its very nature is meaningless. Meanwhile, the task of the great man, according to Nietzsche, consists precisely in giving meaning to the world process, in illuminating with the bright light of consciousness the dark depths of nature.

CHAPTER: III

Nietzsche's views on art of the same period contain the same contradictions. Art is for man a source of consolation in two senses. First, it reveals the metaphysical unity of all beings, the unity of the eternal foundation of the universe; second, it creates a world of beautiful images that distract man from his sufferings and compel him to love life. In works of art, we contemplate eternal, imperishable types of existence. In the sufferings and joys of an individual, in the movements of his thought and feeling, art marks what is typical, those eternal manifestations of life that this individual shares with others of the same kind. The sufferings and joys of some tragic hero, for example, Hamlet, outlive Hamlet himself, because in them is expressed universal life, something that lives in all men and endures in the succession of generations. In aesthetic contemplation, we feel another's emotions, sufferings, and joys as our own; we are imbued with a sense of solidarity with the hero of some novel or tragedy, because we feel that in him and in us the same essence is revealed, the single source of world life which suffers and rejoices in all individuals. In this lies the secret of the pleasure that tragedy affords us. Tragedy usually ends with the death of the hero, and yet from it we carry away a comforting sense of reconciliation and peace: we feel that what has died in the hero continues to live in us; we are filled with the consciousness of eternal life, which triumphs unceasingly over death and after the ruin of one individual is renewed, resurrected in others. "The metaphysical consolation of every true tragedy, – says Nietzsche, – consists in the fact that, in spite of the unceasing change of phenomena, world life is indestructibly powerful and joyful."[38] Tragedy lifts us above our personality, above all that is transient and limited; thereby, it conquers the individual's fear of time and fear of death.[39] This meaning of tragedy was evident to the ancient Greeks: for them, the spirit of tragedy was embodied in the figure of Dionysus-Bacchus, eternally dying and eternally resurrecting. The idea of the unity and eternity of world life, first expressed in the festivals of Dionysus, later underlay all Greek tragedies as their common essence.

This Dionysian motive, however, does not exhaust the content of art in general and of Greek art in particular. In art, we not only perceive the secret of the unity of world essence, but we also rejoice in the endless diversity of individual forms, concrete images, in which this essence is embodied. In the waves of the infinite world, individual beings are born and vanish without cease. The life of each of us is but a passing moment; over us hangs the tragic doom of death; compared with world life, our existence is a phantom, a deceptive dream. What truly exists is not the individual, but only the one and infinite. And yet art makes us rejoice in our existence, desire its continuation. How is this magical effect of art to be explained?

Something similar happens to us in dreams: in dreams, we often know that we are dreaming, but we do not wish to wake because the dream is beautiful. Such also is the effect of art: it creates for us a world of beautiful dreams, enchanting images, and we wish for the continuation of our life; we do not wish to awake from the lie of our individual existence, because we are under enchantment. We, as it were, say to our life: you are a lie, but we want you, because you are beautiful. In this lies the motive of art, which Nietzsche calls Apollonian. Radiant Apollo – god of song and dance – in the eyes of the ancient Greeks embodied that world of beautiful dreams for which it is worth living and rejoicing. Apollo expresses the fundamental idea of the Greek Olympus. In contemplating the beautiful gods, the ancient Greeks forgot suffering and were delivered from the fear of death. Without these gods, life would have been unbearable. In the eyes of the Greeks, these gods justified their existence by the fact that they themselves lived and rejoiced in life.[40] In

Nietzsche's words, the essence of the Apollonian tendency of art comes down to "driving suffering out of nature".[41]

Thus in art, as Nietzsche understands it, two opposing – indeed two contradictory – tendencies are united. In tragic art, it unmasks the lie of individual existence and compels us to rejoice in the very death of the hero; in this lies the Dionysian tendency of art. On the other hand, the Apollonian tendency of art lulls us with beautiful illusion, draws us by the charm of enchantment to deceptive and paltry life. The Dionysian tendency of art is expressed mainly in music, which makes us penetrate into the hidden motive of the world will one in itself; the Apollonian tendency finds expression in plastic art, which immortalizes the beauty of diverse phenomena.[42]

In this conception of art is reflected the struggle of two opposite tendencies of Nietzsche's philosophy and at the same time of two basic inclinations of his nature: the struggle between the pessimism of the thinker and the optimistic dreams of the poet, between the philosophical denial of the meaning of life and the striving to justify it at least "as an aesthetic phenomenon."

Together with Schopenhauer, Nietzsche saw the highest expression of art in music; for in music we are distracted from every external image, we rise above the realm of illusory phenomena in order to contemplate the single essence of the world will, to hearken to that single melody which resounds in everything. For Nietzsche, up to 1876, the supreme embodiment of music was Wagner's creations. In all that exists, he says, Wagner discerned the single world life: with him, everything speaks and nothing is mute. "Having penetrated the secret of morning dawn, of clouds and forest, of mountain peaks and abyss, of night darkness and moonlight, he in all these phenomena discerned their common desire: like us, they want to express themselves in sound. If the philosopher (Schopenhauer) says that there exists a single world will which strives for being in animate and inanimate nature, then the musician adds: and this will at all levels of its being wants to pour itself into sound."[43]

In Wagner's music, Nietzsche discovered the secret of being, and all existence was illumined with higher meaning. It is clear what the loss of this music must have meant for him and what he must have felt when, in 1876, it ceased to delight him. That was the impression of horror; disappointment in Wagner was, for Nietzsche, at the same time, disappointment in himself, in all that had until then been his cherished dream.[44] Later, he saw in the break with Wagner the beginning of his recovery. "Wagner, – he says, – was my sickness"; how severe the sickness was is clear from the fact that Nietzsche regards recovery from it as "the most significant event of his life ".[45]

From this moment, a turning point comes in Nietzsche's philosophical worldview. Disillusioned with Wagner, he felt an instinctive aversion to Schopenhauer, who until then had been his chief philosophical guide.[46] The cause of this reversal lies in the defects and contradictions of that initial standpoint of our philosopher with which we have just become acquainted. This standpoint expresses a transitional state of thought, not yet fully defined and wavering. Nietzsche could not long remain with that twofold evaluation of the significance of the world process and of the individual which he had given in *Schopenhauer as Educator* and other writings of the same period. His hesitations on the question of the purposiveness of world evolution were resolved in the direction of a more precise and more decisive denial of any objective goals in the world, although in his thought, as we shall see, traces of a contradictory attitude toward teleology remained. He parted with Schopenhauer's teaching because it could not answer the question of the meaning of the life of the individual, i.e., precisely the question that from the very beginning was central for him. In philosophy, Nietzsche sought above all a justification of the individual, his active participation in the world process. Meanwhile, from Schopenhauer's standpoint, everything individual as such and every process as such is false, something that ought not to exist and is subject to annulment. Disillusioned with Schopenhauer, Nietzsche felt the shakiness of that "metaphysical consolation" which until then he had sought in philosophy and in art. If philosophy and art testify only to the emptiness and futility of individual existence, if they condemn our life as a lie, then they cannot serve us as a source of consolation. Nietzsche's chief reproach against Wagner's music soon after his disillusionment with it came down to the following: it is "art that denies the harmony of existence and sees it beyond the world",[47] i.e. in that mysterious realm of the "thing-in-itself," where all that exists merges into indifferent unity; there is no place there for diversity and multiplicity of individual beings.

To drive suffering from us and breathe into us vigor, other thoughts and other songs are needed.

CHAPTER: IV

Nietzsche in the Process of Philosophical Search

From 1876, a period of new wanderings of thought opens for Nietzsche. We see him again in search of the ideal of the "true man," for a content that would fill his existence with meaning. Along the way, he experiences the joys of creation. But these passing joys do not drown in him the anxiety and longing for the infinite.

"Once," he says, "a wanderer slammed the door behind him, stopped, and wept. Then he said to himself: this thirst for the true, the real, the genuine, and the certain! How angry I am at it! Why does precisely this dark and passionate pursuer hound me! I long for rest, but it does not allow it. How many things in life draw me to repose! Everywhere on my path, the gardens of Armida await me, hence new pains of parting and new heartaches. I must again strain my tired, wounded foot. And since I must forever go on, I often look back in anger at the most beautiful of what did not hold me, because it could not chain me."[48]

In the process of seeking truth, the thinker detaches himself from everything usual and generally accepted, from all that confines and shackles thought. A wide horizon opens before him, an endless path of wandering. This infinity inspires him with joy and with fear, draws him like an unsolved secret, and weighs on him with uncertainty. These are the very feelings a traveler at sea experiences. "We have left the land and boarded a ship. The gangway is withdrawn, and we have pushed off from the shore. Now, ship, fix your gaze on the distance. Around you is the ocean. True, it does not always rage, and at times it rests as if in a beautiful dream – in silk and gold. But the hour will come, and you will understand that nothing is more terrifying than infinity. Woe to that unlucky bird that felt itself free only to run again against the walls of its cage! Woe to you if in mid-ocean homesickness for the shore comes over you, as if there were more freedom there, and there is no shore anymore."[49]

What Nietzsche describes here is inevitable for anyone who has tasted the charms of free thought. We feel our human limitation most painfully precisely at the moment when, having broken with traditional views, we stand face to face with the abyss and survey with the eye the infinite task of inquiry before us. And longing for the shore makes many return to the already lived-through. Only the fearless and strong do not stop, those whom the storms and dangers of solitary wandering do not frighten.

The thinker's path is anxious and hard; only he can attain the great who can endure great sufferings. In most people, suffering kills energy. "In suffering," says Nietzsche, "I seem to hear the captain's command – take in the sails! There are moments when suffering gives us the signal of an approaching storm; in these moments, we must be able to live with diminished energy, to sail with furled sails. There are, however, people to whom in suffering the opposite command is heard, in whom the very approach of the storm calls forth a surge of pride, an excess of warlike energy, and happiness. In suffering, they live through their most significant moments. These are heroic personalities, great tormentors of mankind, those few, rare people who in their own persons seem like an apology for suffering. "[50]

Only to one who has known the greatest torments are the highest joys, the ecstasies of inspiration, revealed. In Nietzsche's autobiographical notes, there is a vivid description of the ecstatic state he experienced while creating his *Zarathustra*, the work he himself considered his best. It is, in his words, in the full sense an experience of some inner revelation: "Suddenly with extraordinary strength and clarity something becomes vi-sible and tangible to you that seizes you and overturns the whole depth of your being." "You no longer seek, you only listen: you take without asking who gives you. Thought flashes like lightning, at once casting itself into the forms necessary to it; I never had to ponder choice. This is a state of rapture, whose unbelievable tension sometimes resolves in floods of tears."[51] Such moments, however, are a rare exception even in the lives of elect souls, of exceptionally gifted people. The type of man for whom the highest mood is a constant state is absent now and can be born only in the future. "For such people," says Nietzsche, "the whole of life will turn into an unceasing motion between height and depth and will be an unceasing sensation of height and depth: they will experience a feeling of continuous ascent and at the same time as if resting on clouds."[52]

In everything Nietzsche writes, we are struck by his ardent temperament, the extraordinary force of life bubbling up. Both suffering and joy are felt by him with doubled energy.[53] He makes on life such heightened demands that nothing can satisfy them. His passion for knowledge turns into greed. He himself says of himself that he has an insatiable soul, "which wants to possess everything, to see with the eyes of a multitude of individuals and grasp with their hands as with its own, to extend its dominion even over times past; it wishes to lose nothing of what can belong to it. Oh, flame of my greed! Oh, if only I could be reborn as hundreds of beings! Whoever has not experienced from his own experience the force of this sigh does not know what the passion for knowledge is!"[54]

The reverse side of this thirst for life and knowledge is perpetual dissatisfaction. The passing joys of creation appear and vanish like lightning, and in this incessant burning of life, the philosopher can find neither calm nor lasting happiness. Through Nietzsche's cheerfulness shines a deep sadness, which forms the basis of his mood. Already in 1874, he repeats after Schopenhauer: "Happiness in life is impossible; the highest man can attain is an existence filled with heroism."[55] At that time, music sweetened for Nietzsche the sufferings of life and served him as a source of consolation. Later, five years after his disillusionment with Wagner, he writes: "The greatest musician for me is the one who knows only one sorrow-the sorrow of the highest happiness; such musicians have not yet been born."[56]

Short-lived moments of happiness do not cancel the deep grief that forms the very foundation of our existence. Hence, the peculiar attitude of exceptional individuals toward happiness. "People of deep sorrow betray themselves in happiness. They treat it as though they would like to smother and strangle it – out of jealousy: they know too well that it will soon betray them."[57]

The instability of happiness expresses the general mark of all that is in time: everything in the world is process, everything flows, and nothing abides. Our unhappiness is rooted in the mismatch of our will with the conditions of our existence. Life reaches its highest expression in our striving to imprint the character of permanence on the general flow of things, to preserve being in the stream of phenomena.[58] But we are powerless to stop time, and in this lies the source of our suffering. "I gave a name to my suffering," says Nietzsche, "and call it a dog: it is as faithful, as importunate, shameless, clever, and as entertaining as any other dog. I can dominate it and pour my vexation on it: the very thing that others do to dogs, servants, and women."[59] Since happiness cannot be attained in life, its highest rule must be the heroism of the personality going against its highest suffering and its highest hope.[60] The mark of true greatness lies not in the ability to endure suffering–perfected even in women and slaves – but in not being absorbed in it, not being destroyed by it.[61] This feat is especially hard for those few who are fully aware of what they are experiencing and therefore possess a refined sensitivity to every sting of life.

Most people rush through life in a kind of intoxication and

as if tumoring down a staircase, endlessly stumbling and falling. "Thanks to our intoxication," says Nietzsche, "you do not break your limbs in the process: your muscles are so slack and your consciousness so clouded that you do not feel, as we do, the full hardness of these stone steps. For us, life is a greater danger: we are made of glass; woe to us when we bump, and all is lost for us when we fall."[62] From this standpoint, Nietzsche understands the charm of that voluntary blindness which at times restrains us from looking into the future. This is expressed in the following aphorism: "My thoughts," said the wanderer to his shadow, "must show me where I stand; but they must not blurt out to me where I am going. I love the uncertainty of the future and do not want to suffer from impatience and from anticipation of the promised things."[63]

Hardest of all for the thinker are those moments when he is ready to lose faith in himself, when doubt assails him about the truth he seeks, the object of his search, and the goal of his life. Nietzsche has an acceptable aphorism – one of the pearls of his poetic creation – where he compares the highest aim of his and of all human striving with the meaningless play of sea waves.

"With what fury this wave rushes on: as if it hoped to achieve something! With what terrifying haste it creeps into every crevice of the coastal rocks, as though it wanted to warn someone, as though something precious, very precious, were hidden there. Now it returns somewhat slower, yet still foaming with excitement. Has disappointment seized it? Did it find what it sought? Or does it only pretend to be disappointed? But now comes another wave, still more fearful and furious than the first; it also seems filled with secrets and with passion for the quest of treasures. There live the waves, and thus we live, we who will – I have nothing to add. Is it so? You do not trust me? You are angry, beautiful monsters! Do you fear that I will betray your secret? Be it so! Be angry at me, raise your green and terrible masses as high as you can; build a wall between me and the sun, just so, as now. Already, the whole world is drowning in green shimmer and green lightning. Continue as much as you like, you proud ones, roar with passion and rage, plunge again into the depths, scatter your emerald into the abyss, toss endlessly spray and foaming spume; for me all is well, for in every way you are good, and all inclines me toward you. And how can I betray your secret! For, listen to me closely – I know you and your secret, I know your kind. You and I belong to one and the same kind; you and I have one common secret."[64]

In reading this aphorism, the question inevitably arises: can a man who so vividly depicts the futility of all striving believe in his own life task and in the truth of his teaching? The question cannot be resolved either affirmatively or negatively. Nietzsche is too complex a nature, and in his soul, opposite tendencies clash. Fiery faith in himself and in the new word he is called to speak to mankind inspires him in moments of creation and gives him strength to live, but this faith constantly collides with tormenting doubts. Alongside passages testifying to his faith in reason, we also find in his writings those in which he mocks reason. In the heat of polemic against modern idols, doubt suddenly seizes him about his own negation; he stops and asks himself: but is not my standpoint also only a mode of self-soothing?[65] He, preacher of a new life ideal, at times asks himself whether an opposition exists between conviction and falsehood?[66] In his search for the true and the certain, he, as we shall later see, comes among other things to a sophistic denial of the true and the certain altogether. What value under such conditions can any teaching and teaching office have? Nietzsche states outright that a true teacher is one who takes things seriously, including himself, only in relation to his pupils.[67]

As we shall see later, Nietzsche does not in vain recognize himself as the continuator and successor of the most gifted of the ancient sophists, Protagoras.[68] But his doubts about himself lie in a deeper and more serious source than sophistry. He possesses great, very great artistic talent, and at times the artist in him prevails over the philosopher. In these moments, he rises above his own teaching, painfully conscious of the impotence of any word and any thought to express that great secret which he instinctively feels in the mute grandeur of nature and its beauty.

No translation can convey the marvelous charm of the description of the evening over the sea that we find in his *Dawn*. Nietzsche depicts here the scene of universal silence of nature after the sun has set over the sea. The sea grows still, shining with a whitish glow. The sky is silent too, playing the eternal play of rainbow colors of evening twilight; silent are the coastal stones and cliffs jutting into the sea, as if seeking in it a place of solitude. This majestic silence of the elements is both beautiful and terrible; the mute beauty of nature seems to mock thought and shame the word. Silence fills the heart: "It receives with horror the revelation of a new truth: it too smiles when lips utter something amid this beauty; for it, the treachery of silence becomes sweet. Speech and even thought become hateful to me: do I not hear in every word error, self-delusion, deception! – O evening, O sea! You evil teachers! You teach man so that he ceases to be man. Must he give himself to you and become like you, pale, radiant, mute, and majestic? Must he find peace above himself and rise above himself?"[69]

Nietzsche, as an artist, feels in the beauty of the universe a mystery that surpasses all that is human, exposing as vulgar every word of ours, and he is dissatisfied with his philosophical works. Every thought expressed, every word written immediately loses for him its charm, becomes lifeless and slack, echoes a commonplace truth and a banality. Most curious is how he explains this phenomenon. Our human word, he says, like the painter's brush, can grasp and depict only what lends itself to depiction. We forever write only what is already beginning to wither and lose its fragrance; only the birds already tired of flight fall into our hands, those that can be caught by hands, our hands.

We can immortalize only what can no longer live long, all that has already become flaccid and weary.[70] Over Nietzsche's creativity hangs that mood which he himself calls "the melancholy of everything finished: having completed the building, we suddenly notice that in doing so we have learned something which we absolutely should have known earlier, before beginning the building. This eternal and unbearable 'Too late'."[71]

What has been said about sorrow as the basis of Nietzsche's mood seems contradicted by the fact that he is a preacher of cheerfulness; he wants to inspire the reader with gaiety, vigor, and we shall still have to reckon with this preaching. But this "joy of life" in his mouth is rather a prescription, a counsel to himself and others, than a depiction of actual mood. Through this "joy of life," we feel the yearning for the unattainable ideal of true life. It is the cheerfulness of a man who wants to be cheerful in order to conceal from himself and from others the deepest secret of his sufferings. It is a comedy hard to maintain throughout a whole life, and Nietzsche, in the end, betrays himself. There are, he says, "cheerful people" who use cheerfulness to mislead others: they do not want to be understood. In such cases, cheerfulness is a mask, and "others" must avoid indiscreet curiosity, must respect the "alien mask".[72] Everything profound shuns indiscreet glances and "loves a mask".[73] "Every deep thinker," we read elsewhere, "fears more being understood than being misunderstood. In the latter case, perhaps, his vanity suffers, but in the former – his sympathy for others, which always says: 'Ah, why should you suffer what I have suffered!'."[74] That is why Nietzsche sees in the very process of writing a way of concealing his essence, that "mask" which he regards as a necessary attribute of all philosophy.[75]

For us, of course, what is most interesting is not Nietzsche's mask, but precisely what he covers with it: the image of the wanderer, the homeless vagabond of thought, who has gone around the universe, has not found what he sought, and has nowhere to lay his head. In this image, which returns incessantly in his writings, it is not hard to recognize Nietzsche himself.

"Wanderer, who are you?! I see you making your way without scorn, without love; with an unreadable gaze, sad and moist, you are like a leaden weight that has resurfaced into the light from the depths. What did you seek there, insatiable one? I see your breast that does not sigh, your lips hiding disgust, and your hand slowly grasping. Who are you, and what did you do? Rest here! This place is hospitable to all. Rest, and whoever you may be, say what you now desire; what do you need for rest? Only name it, I offer you all that I have." – "For rest, for rest?! What word did you utter, curious one! But give me, however, I beg you…" – "What, what, speak at last!" – "A mask, another mask!"[76]

CHAPTER: V

In Nietzsche's eyes, the mask expresses the philosopher's need for seclusion: he wants to remain alone with his thought and values the mask precisely because it separates, sets distance[77] between him and his neighbor. What can the neighbor give him with his suffering: what use is the compassion of those who themselves suffer?[78] In the end, all men are infected with the infirmity of universal vanity, and therefore their participation can not ease but only intensify the torment of the "wanderer." Solitude, Zarathustra teaches, is of two kinds: it is either the flight of the sick, or flight from the sick.[79] Nietzsche's flight from society was conditioned both by the fact that he himself was ill and by the fact that he considered others ill. In the search for truth, the neighbor is for him not a helper but an obstacle, or at best a "soft bed" – a means of temporary self-soothing.[80] The true philosopher Nietzsche imagines in the image of a hermit – Zarathustra, who lives in a cave on mountain heights inaccessible to men. He is an exile who in no "fatherland" feels at home and loves as homeland only the world of the future of mankind, not the "land of fathers," but the not-yet-opened "land of children".[81] In the "land of fathers," in contemporary humanity, he is repelled by the low standard level: "Everywhere," he says, "I see low gates: whoever is like me may pass through, but he must forever stoop".[82] The interests of the masses are absolutely alien to him, and therefore he feels even lonelier among men than away from them: solitude for him is by no means the same as loneliness.[83]

Avoiding men, the philosopher at the same time needs them. In his relation to men, he experiences an unceasing oscillation between aversion and attraction, for all of Nietzsche's philosophizing is, first, a longing for the sure and steadfast, which should fill life with content, and second, a search for the true man. That is why Zarathustra cannot remain long in the solitude of his cave. He now ascends to the cloud-piercing mountain peaks, now descends to the plains inhabited by men, and, disappointed, again returns to his cave. In these unending ascents and descents passes Zarathustra's whole life: his wanderings must continue without end, because they cannot reach the goal. The tragedy of his situation lies in the fact that, despising man, he is compelled at the same time to seek in him support for his hope.

Having reached the highest summit in his wandering, Zarathustra sees before him a sudden abyss. His head spins, and in his heart two impulses struggle: fear of the precipice and striving upward; not height is terrible, the abyss is terrible.

"Ah, friends," he says, "do you divine the twofold will of my heart? My precipice and my danger consist in this, that my gaze is directed upward, but my hand wishes to cling and to lean upon the abyss.

To men my will clings; I chained myself with chains to men, for I feel an attraction upward, to the overman: thither tends my will. And for that I live blindly among men, as though I did not know them, in order that my hand may not wholly lose their faith in the immutable."[84]

In the search for the immutable Nietzsche clings to man, but in the life of mankind, shifting and fluid, he finds only one immutable and certain thing – death, which dogs our steps. "With happiness mixed with sadness," he says, "I live amid the overcrowded street's confusion of human voices and desires: how much joy, impatience, desire manifests in every moment of the day, how much thirst for life and intoxication with it. And yet what silence soon awaits all these noisy and life-thirsting ones! Behind each stands his shadow, his dark companion of life. All that is happening is as in the last moment before a ship's departure into the ocean. We have more to say to one another than ever before. The ocean, silent as a desert, impatiently awaits amid the general clamor, so greedy and certain of its prey. And everyone thinks that all that has been hitherto is either altogether nothing or insignificant, and the nearest future is everything! Each wishes to be first in this future, and yet death and the stillness of the grave are the only certain and common thing that awaits all. How strange that this only certainty has almost no effect upon men, and that the thought that all are bound by the brotherhood of death stands furthest from them. I am happy to see that men do not at all wish to think out the thought of death. I would gladly do something so that the thought of life might appear to them a hundredfold more worthy of thought."[85]

The ordinary man does not reflect on his end, but simply sets the thought of it aside, directing his attention to other things. But for the philosopher, who sees in the question of the purpose and meaning of existence his fundamental task, the thought of death acquires central significance. All of Nietzsche's philosophy is, in essence, an attempt to overcome the fear of death and to answer the question of whether life is worth living at all. In what follows, we shall see how he dealt with this task.

CHAPTER: VI

Nietzsche's Doctrine in the Final Stage of Its Development: His View of the Essence of the World Process

Nietzsche's philosophy is, first of all, a perfect atheism; but its peculiar feature lies not in this, but in the fact that he dared to think his atheism through to the end, to derive from it all its logical consequences. He does not belong to that common type of philosopher of our time for whom questions related to religion are dismissed as finally resolved. On the contrary, these questions form the very center around which his thought revolves. The most interesting side of his philosophy lies in the fact that he understood atheism as the fundamental problem of his entire life and thought. Subjecting modern culture, intellectual and moral life to critical analysis, he became convinced above all of the superficiality of modern unbelief: on the one hand, modern thought appears essentially irreligious; on the other hand, modern humanity is unable to let go of the old traditional evaluation of life, of a whole series of ethical formulas inseparably tied to faith. In its denial of religion, our age has remained halfway: our entire life still rests on religious assumptions, on unconscious beliefs. And so Nietzsche resolved to trace and reject these assumptions, to throw overboard everything that is in one way or another connected to them.

The task is set before him in this way: "God is dead," but people continue to live as if the news of His death has not yet reached their consciousness: "After the death of Buddha, his shadow was still shown for centuries in a cave – a huge, dreadful shadow. God is dead, but as the human race is constituted, there may still be caves for thousands of years in which His shadow will be shown. And we-we must still defeat His shadow."[86]

From this point of view, the whole world must appear in a new light. Consistent atheism must, first of all, renounce teleology: every doctrine that attempts to explain the development of nature and humanity from the point of view of any final purposes must be rejected as a remnant of outlived beliefs.[87] The concept of purpose is the first in which Nietzsche sees the shadow of God; it has nothing to do with reality and is entirely our invention.

Whoever takes this standpoint must recognize that "the world is chaos." The philosophy of our days loves to depict the world as an "organism," as a "living whole," but such an understanding of the universe contains a remnant of the notion of its purposiveness. Where there is an organism, there is purpose. But what can the universe have in common with an organism? The distinguishing feature of all organic life is nourishment, growth, and reproduction. But how can the universe grow? How can it reproduce? In relation to the world as a whole, the organism is something derivative and late, accidental and rare; it is the mold of the Earth, a growth on the Earth's crust; and we want to see in this growth the essence of the universe, something universal and eternal?

The entire organic world is nothing more than a happy accident, a transient phenomenon of our earthly planet; and in relation to the world as a whole, our planet itself and our entire astral system are nothing more than an accident. The regular, periodic rotation of the celestial bodies is by no means a universal law of matter's movement: at the very sight of the Milky Way, the question arises, isn't motion disorderly, formless, a general rule? The astral system in which we live is nothing more than an exception; meanwhile, it is precisely this that makes our organic world possible – an exception among exceptions. In the world process as a whole, there is no beauty, no order, no form: it is a meaningless and mad process. To say that life is essential in nature is to falsely liken nature to man: nature has no aspirations, no ideals; for it, life is no different from death; in it, the living is no more than a variety of the dead – and a very rare one at that. Let us not speak of the perfection of nature, of its wisdom and goodness, or conversely, of its malice and irrationality. Nature is entirely alien to our oppositions of good and evil, rational and senseless: all that is human is alien to it, and it has no intention of imitating man.

Nietzsche once saw in man the ultimate goal of nature, its hope and salvation. Now he rejects this idea as a false attempt to humanize nature, to obscure it with the "shadow of God." Amid the general disorder of the universe, what is man with his reason? A small, eccentric variety of animal, doomed, like all living things, to a brief existence; the life of this variety is a fleeting moment, an adventure of the earthly planet, leaving no noticeable trace in it; the planet itself is a gap between two states of nothingness – an event without plan, without reason, self-consciousness, or will, a manifestation of the worst kind of necessity – a stupid necessity. It would be in vain to think that man is the crown of creation: if we say that all other creatures are on the same level of perfection as he, even this may grant him too much; in comparison with other beings, man is the most unsuccessful of animals – the most diseased, the most deviated from his instincts, though perhaps also the most interesting.

Humanity is not an improvement of nature, not a step forward in its development, because in the world as a whole, there is no movement forward, no progress, no regress in the sense of change for better or worse.[88] The illusion of world progress rests on the illusion of a world goal. Our habit of assuming a purpose at the foundation of existence constantly makes us think that the world is moving toward some state of perfection, that the present exists only for the future. But if the world had any goal, it would already have been reached; if it were capable of a "final state" of perfection, it would have arrived long ago, for the world's movement has been going on for an infinite time. The very fact of the uninterrupted flow of phenomena proves that the world has no purpose and, consequently, no end: it dies constantly and is born again endlessly, feeding on its own excrement; it flows eternally and is incapable of freezing in any state; there is nothing transient in it, nothing eternal except the process of infinite flow itself. It would be wrong to think that in its development the world does not repeat itself: the absence of repetitions would imply a purpose, an intention in world life. If the world process were a conscious, meaningful one, then each of its stages would represent a definite step toward perfection, an achieved result not subject to repetition.

But since the world process is not a striving toward a goal, it represents circular rather than progressive motion. Having reached a specific limit in its development, the world again returns to its starting point. It presents a picture of unceasing and infinite repetition.

Here Nietzsche preaches exactly what the devil says in Dostoevsky's novel in the dream of the sick Ivan Karamazov: "You're still thinking about our present-day Earth. But perhaps the present-day Earth has already repeated itself a billion times; well, it lived out its life, froze over, cracked, crumbled, decomposed into its elements; then again the waters above the firmament, then again a comet, again the sun, again from the sun – the Earth – this development, perhaps, has repeated itself endlessly, and always in the exact same form, down to the smallest detail. An utterly indecent boredom…"

What Dostoevsky portrays as the nightmarish delirium of the sick Ivan Fyodorovich, for Nietzsche, bears the stamp of genuine reality. And he, like Dostoevsky's devil, teaches that everything in the world repeats itself, down to the smallest detail – Sirius, the spider, and every event of our lives in every given minute. But unlike the devil, Nietzsche does not consider it possible to call this cycle of life "boring" or "stupid," since our human notions of reason or absurdity cannot at all serve as characteristics of the world as a whole. Nietzsche's article "On the Eternal Return of Things" was written in 1881, that is, immediately after Dostoevsky completed *The Brothers Karamazov*. The coincidence of ideas and even expressions here, however, is accidental, since at that time Nietzsche could not have been familiar with Dostoevsky's novel, which had not yet been translated into any foreign language.

Nietzsche attempts to prove the doctrine of eternal return. He sees in it a necessary consequence of the law of conservation of energy. This law states that energy or force does not arise nor perish. World energy does not decrease or increase; consequently, it is forever a fixed, unchanging, and therefore finite quantity. But once world energy is quantitatively finite, then the number of its manifestations, the combinations in which it appears, cannot be unlimited. If this world consists of a definite amount of forces and a definite number of force centers, then in the course of its movement, it must repeat a definite and therefore calculable number of combinations. This number may be enormous and – from our human point of view – immeasurable; but in infinite time, all possible combinations must be exhausted; hence, over infinite time, every possible combination must repeat itself; moreover, it must repeat itself an infinite number of times; and since, at every given moment of the universe's existence, infinite time has already elapsed, then all possible combinations of world forces have already been repeated an infinite number of times and will be repeated just as infinitely. But since all possible combinations must occur before each specific one can return again, and since each given combination necessarily determines the entire sequence of following combinations, the world process presents itself as a cycle, in which absolutely identical sequences of phenomena and events eternally return. This is an eternally revolving wheel, a play of forces, continuing into infinity. Suppose, at a particular moment in time, an absolutely new combination, never before seen, suddenly appears in the world, or that some previously existing combination never returns. That would mean that there has been either an increase or a decrease in the total amount of world energy, but both are contrary to the law of conservation or constancy of world energy; therefore, neither is possible.

Nietzsche compares the life of the universe and our human life to a process occurring in an hourglass: when all the sand has passed from one chamber to the other, the glass is turned over, and the whole process begins again – and so on into eternity. When our life is restored in this cycle, we will find the same sorrow and the same joy, meet the same friend and foe in the same place, the same sunbeam and the same blade of grass in the field. Every one of our thoughts has already been thought billions of times, and every one of our feelings has already been felt billions of times. Between our present life and its future return will pass billions and billions of years, but compared to infinite time, these billions are like a second, and we will not even notice the gap, for during the intermission between our two existences, our consciousness will fade.

"You think you will rest for a long time before your rebirth," Nietzsche says. "Do not be deceived: between the last moment of your consciousness and the first glimpse of new life, no time will pass at all; the transition occurs with the speed of lightning, though living beings measure it in billions of years – or may not be able to measure it at all. As soon as there is no intellect, alternation in time and the absence of time become one and the same."[89]

Nietzsche emphasizes the idea that his understanding of the world process is a necessary consequence of the atheistic point of view: if there is no other, higher force above the world directing it toward a goal, if there is no divine will above it, then world movement cannot be anything other than a process of recurrence...[90]

CHAPTER: VII

The Structure of the Universe in Its Relation to Man

No matter what Nietzsche speaks about, man, his task, and goal are always at the forefront for him. The primary interest of the doctrine of eternal return, from the very beginning, lies for him in the question: what new does this doctrine bring into human life? How should it affect our mood and activity? What are its practical consequences?

These consequences appear boundless: from the moment, Nietzsche says, that this thought first flashed by, all the colors, all the lighting of our life change, and a new era of history begins.[91]

First of all, for man, eternal return means a kind of immortality, eternal life. But this is not eternal life in another and better world, but precisely in this world, in which we now languish and suffer. Can such immortality serve man as a source of consolation and joy? Nietzsche rightly sees in it a new trial and a new torment: "The highest that is possible for us," he says, "is to be able to endure our immortality".[92]

Indeed, the immortality in question here means above all the eternity of suffering, the futility of all attempts to improve our surroundings and to perfect ourselves. All human life is a striving to rise above the present moment, a search for other and better values than those we possess; under these conditions, what could be more terrible for us than the realization that the present moment is fated to repeat itself an infinite number of times, that all the time to pass between this moment and its return in the future will flash by like lightning! Can we rejoice that our entire life is an endless and eternal pouring from the empty into the void? Should not this new doctrine ultimately kill all energy within us?

Dostoevsky in his novel – *The House of the Dead* says, among other things, that for a person there is nothing more tormenting than pointless work: if we were forced to repeat one and the same series of meaningless actions for a long time, for example, to carry a pile of sand from place to place, this would be for us a kind of hellish torture. Nietzsche, who compares our existence to the process in an hourglass, essentially asserts that our whole life is like this. If we add to this that even our death must be repeated an innumerable number of times, then the return of all that exists becomes for us that eternal hell from which even suicide does not save.

Nietzsche himself fears the possible consequences of his doctrine: perhaps, he says, it will turn out to be deadly precisely for the best people, for those who demand the highest from life! Will it not serve as a comfort for the worst? For ultimately, it may flatter the flat instincts of the masses who are content with the ordinary: with animal existence. The higher, better people will be the last to come to terms with the newly discovered truth: in this, Nietzsche says, lies the suffering of those who love the truth.[93]

Man wants to live meaningfully, rationally; in this lies what is specifically human, what distinguishes us from other creatures. "Man," Nietzsche says, "gradually became a fantastical animal, for whom, in addition to what other animals need, one more condition of existence is necessary: man must now and then know why he exists; his kind cannot thrive without periodically arising trust in life. And the human race will always, from time to time, declare: 'There is something that can no longer be ridiculed at all'."[94] Nietzsche explains the constant rebirth of the doctrine of life's purpose in religions and philosophical systems by this; in this doctrine he sees a "delusion necessary for the preservation of the human race".[95]

Kill in man the belief in his goal, and you kill in him the man. To reconcile oneself with existence in which one sees no goal or meaning means ultimately to renounce reason, for every movement of our reason presupposes a goal toward which it is directed: aimlessness is the same as irrationality. Our entire will rests on the same assumption: to want consciously means to presume that there is something unconditionally valuable, unconditionally worthy of desire.

Faith in the goal of life – this is the sun that illuminates our existence; but to believe in a goal means to believe in reason as the beginning and end of what exists, that is, ultimately, to believe in God. Nietzsche feels that religious need lies at the root of our being, and in this lies the secret torment of his atheism. In denying purpose, he is fully aware of what the loss of God means for man.

"Have you not heard," he says, "of that madman who lit a lantern in the bright morning and ran to the marketplace, shouting without ceasing: 'I seek God, I seek God!' Because many unbelievers were standing around there, he provoked much laughter. 'Did he get lost?' said one. 'Did he run away like a child?' said another. 'Or is he hiding? Is he afraid of us? Has he gone to sea? Emigrated?' – thus they shouted and laughed. The madman sprang into their midst and pierced them with his eyes. 'Where has God gone?' he cried. 'I will tell you! We have killed him – you and I! We are all his murderers. But how have we done this? How were we able to drink up the sea? Who gave us the sponge to wipe away the whole horizon? What were we doing when we unchained this Earth from its sun? Whither is it moving now? Whither are we moving now? Away from all suns? Are we not plunging continually? Backward, sideward, forward, in all directions? Is there still above and below? Are we not wandering as through an infinite nothing? Do we not feel the breath of empty space? Has it not become colder? Does not night come on continually, darker and darker? Mustn't lanterns be lit in the morning? Do we not hear the gravediggers who are burying God? Do we not smell the divine decay? – for even gods decay! God is dead. God remains dead."

What is most striking in these lines is that the atheist Nietzsche evidently sympathizes with the madman. The madman, for whom the loss of God is the loss of the sun, and life without God is a wandering in the darkness of eternal night, shames the crowd of indifferent and frivolous people who do not realize the meaning and consequences of their denial.

Amid the silence of the astonished crowd, the madman finally threw his lantern to the ground, shattered it, and said: "I came too early, my time has not yet come. This tremendous event is still on its way, still wandering; it has not yet reached the ears of men. Lightning and thunder need time; the light of the stars needs time; deeds need time, even after they are done, to be seen and heard. This deed is still further from them than the farthest stars – and yet they have done it themselves."[96]

CHAPTER: VIII

If religious belief in a "purpose of life" is by its very nature a necessary condition for the existence of the human race, then for Nietzsche, this means that an error lies hidden in these conditions and that new conditions of existence must be created for man. That sun which fills people's lives with warmth and light has gone dark for him, but how is he to live without the sun! Where is he to find peace, and how to justify his existence? "I no longer seek anything," he says, "I myself want to create a sun for myself".[97]

In the early period of his philosophical activity, Nietzsche sought metaphysical consolation and found it in contemplation of a single eternal essence, that unconditional, actual being which "can no longer be denied." Now he comes to the conclusion that above the world of appearances there is nothing unconditional, "nothing that cannot be ridiculed." For him, there is no longer any metaphysical consolation. And he now seeks consolation not beyond, but on this side of the universe,[98] in the realm of the moving and changeable.

He wants to find consolation in the very idea of eternal return, which he considers fatal for man and for humanity. But to accept this idea as consolation, all our views on life and its aims must be changed: for this, a "revaluation of all values" is necessary – and, first of all, a renunciation of all morality.

That pessimistic or, as Nietzsche says, "nihilistic" point of view which condemns the world and considers life unbearable, is the result of a mistaken application of the demands of reason – especially our moral demands – to the world as a whole. Our reason looks for purpose and meaning everywhere, and thus we condemn the world because it has no meaning, because our category of purpose is inapplicable to it. We seek unity in the world as a whole and again condemn it because we find nothing in it but a chaotic plurality of phenomena, nothing corresponding to our idea of unity. We apply our demands for truth and goodness to life, and as a result, we devalue life, because the surrounding reality is full of lies and evil, because it appears to be in complete contradiction to our moral demands. In short, pessimism condemns the universe because it cannot withstand the critique of our ideals, because it contradicts our values.[99]

From this follows the conclusion: to overcome pessimism, we must renounce our false categories of reason; to love life, we must, like external nature, stand "beyond good and evil," break the tablets of our values.

From the Christian point of view, the whole world lies in evil: it is condemned because it is under the power of sin. The first consequence of denying purpose in the world is the denial of sin, the justification of the world. If there is no higher will above the universe, and therefore no higher ideal or criterion, then there is no sin in it: all that exists is sinless and innocent. If, in our evaluation of nature, we have risen above the opposition of good and evil, then all indignation at the disorder of the universe, all condemnation of life, falls away on its own. All things are "baptized in the source of eternity," all dwell "beyond good and evil."

Our ideas of good and evil are like clouds that darken our vision; let us rise above these clouds! Then nothing will prevent us from contemplating the clear, pure sky and enjoying it. The curse that weighs upon life will turn into a blessing for us,[100] evil will cease to provoke our disgust – it will no longer require justification. The cruelty of nature, the wild manifestations of animal passion in it and in man, will no longer be a subject of horror for us.[101]

This attitude toward external nature, in Nietzsche's view, is not an act of submission or humility. Humility is an act of self-denial of the human will: it presupposes a higher will above us, to which we submit. If such a higher will does not exist, then we have no one to submit to, no one before whom to humble ourselves. By stepping beyond good and evil, we thereby acknowledge ourselves as part of almighty nature. This is no longer self-denial, but, on the contrary, the highest act of self-affirmation by a will that thirsts for life.

By recognizing that there is nothing higher above the world, we thereby deify nature and ourselves. By denying any life beyond the universe, we thereby affirm that it is this world, this life, that is divine. We bless what exists, pronounce upon it our "amen," our "let it be".[102]

This attitude toward the universe bears the mark of a kind of religiosity, but not Christian religiosity, but rather pagan. Nietzsche openly declares himself a pagan and opposes Christ, the Greek god Dionysus – Bacchus. Christ, crucified on the cross, is a symbol of life's denial. In contrast, Dionysus embodies intoxication with life, delight in it. This is the same idea Nietzsche had expressed in his youthful work *The Birth of Tragedy*. Now, as then, the image of Dionysus personifies for our philosopher his hope and consolation. Dionysus for him is the symbol of the eternal cycle of world life, the eternal return of all that exists, the joyful manifestation of the almighty force of life, endlessly dying and rising again.[103]

To find consolation in the cult of Dionysus, for Nietzsche, means to rejoice in the very disorder of the universe, in its chaos and senselessness. It is precisely in this that our philosopher sees the sign of the "higher man" and the highest disposition. Nietzsche not only reconciles himself with life as it was and is: he wants it to remain so for all eternity, he demands the infinite repetition not only of himself, not only of individual scenes from the world's comedy, but of the entire comedy from beginning to end.[104]

Partial affirmation or denial of world life appears to be extremely illogical. Every phenomenon, every event, is necessarily conditioned by the entire preceding series of world phenomena and, in turn, determines, as one of the conditions, the entire subsequent series. Therefore, if we desire anything in life, we thereby desire world life in its entirety; conversely, if we deny anything, we thereby deny everything.[105]

To desire life thus means to desire suffering and falsehood, which are fatally connected with it. But how can all of this become desirable to us? This is possible only for those rare few who are capable of rising to the "tragic disposition." The essence of this disposition lies in the fact that we look at the world as a beautiful and engaging spectacle: drama, danger, suffering, and even death are necessary; all of this gives it interest and serves as a source of enjoyment.

The beauty of the world as a whole, which uplifts and delights us, according to Nietzsche, is not something inherent in the nature of things: things in themselves are neither beautiful nor ugly; beauty is brought into them by our aesthetic contemplation, by our artistic creativity. But without this lie of art, life would be unbearable: our existence can only be justified to us as an aesthetic phenomenon. In science, reality appears before us without embellishment, in all its nakedness; scientific analysis convinces us that our entire life rests on illusion, that at the root of all our feelings and self-consciousness lies sheer self-deception; to live with this truth would be impossible for us. Scientific understanding of the world would lead to disgust with life and suicide if it did not find its counterbalance in art. Art gives us the power to distance ourselves from ourselves, to look at life and at our own existence from a certain perspective, in artistic detachment; and from a distance, it seems beautiful; all the sorrow of our being is transformed into an aesthetic phenomenon; we can laugh, cry, and rejoice.[106]

From this point of view, life itself becomes a kind of art. Our existence lacks an objective purpose, but creativity is within our power: we can create purpose and values for ourselves, shape our life in such a way that it produces the impression of beauty – that is, becomes an aesthetic phenomenon. We are destined to live forever – that is, to return eternally in the periodic renewal of all that exists. Let us then live so that our life truly bears the stamp of eternity; let us think and feel in such a way that we could desire the eternal return of each of our thoughts and each of our feelings: this is precisely what the art of living consists in.

Once a person becomes the creator of his own life, the news of the eternal return of things sounds to him like great consolation and joy: he realizes that he is creating something imperishable, eternal; he thus feels himself saved from the law of universal flux and universal death.[107] That minute is immortal, says Nietzsche, in which I created the doctrine of eternal return: for the sake of that minute, I can endure the eternal return.[108]

To endure this thought requires, in general, a superhuman strength. Therefore, Nietzsche believes that it is destined to bring about a revolution in human history: those races for whom the doctrine of eternal return proves unbearable are doomed in advance to perish; conversely, those who accept it as good news are destined to rule.[109] The collapse of religion will have fatal significance for all weak, degenerating human types: having lost belief in the purpose of existence, most people will gradually sink into apathy, cease to strive for anything, and begin to die out. In the end, only those people of strong fiber will remain on the stage – those capable of rejoicing in the eternal repetition of their existence; among these people, a social condition may arise that no utopian has yet dared to dream of.[110]

Thus, the doctrine of eternal return prepares humanity for transition to a new type – the overman, who is destined to triumph in the future; this, for Nietzsche, is the source of new joy. From this perspective, he welcomes the emergence of those pessimistic doctrines that take away from weak people the desire to live. Pessimism, he says, is a useful and powerful tool in the hands of the philosopher; it is the hammer that shatters all that is unfit for life, that clears from the path the degenerate and dying races, paving the way for a new order of life.[111]

CHAPTER: IX

Before proceeding to the exposition of further sections of Nietzsche's teachings, it is necessary to look back on the path traveled and critically examine what has already been presented. We have seen that the starting point of Nietzsche's philosophy is atheism; its ultimate result is the negation of man, which takes two forms – a theoretical judgment and a practical prescription.

The theoretical negation amounts to stating a fact. If this sensually perceived world is the only reality, if there is no other, higher reality above it, then there is nothing that would elevate man above his surrounding environment: he is no more than a phenomenon of nature, equivalent to its other phenomena, or more precisely, equally valueless as them. From the absence of God above the world, Nietzsche concludes that there is neither above nor below; from this point of view, of course, it is absurd to see man as something "higher" compared to other creatures: like them, he is a manifestation of general senselessness.

The meaning of these theoretical judgments, thus, boils down to denying man as something special within and opposed to external nature. But the negation of man also appears in Nietzsche in the form of a practical demand, an imperative. Man must renounce the religious assumptions of his consciousness, the illusion of purpose, everything specifically human, and become like external nature – "beyond good and evil."

It is evident that here we are dealing with a fundamental contradiction in Nietzsche's point of view. The opposition between man and external nature appears to him simultaneously as something nonexistent and as something tangible but improper, to be eliminated.

If man is a phenomenon of nature just as necessary as all other phenomena of world energy, then to address any demands to him is just as absurd as preaching to stones. It is especially absurd to demand that he become like nature, return to it, if he essentially already is a part of that nature.

Nietzsche repeatedly expresses himself in this vein: he mocks those moralists who want to improve humanity. Their demand that man become different from what he is seems incredibly comical, he says; after all, man is a partial manifestation of the "universal fate." To tell him, "You must change," means demanding a change in the whole world – not only in the present, but also in the past, since man's "present" is the result of the entire past of the universe. If there is no purpose over the cosmos or over man, then there is no standard by which anything can be condemned or human life directed toward something better.[112]

Such is the viewpoint of consistent immoralism, but the whole issue is that Nietzsche does not remain – and cannot remain – consistent in his immoralism. One of the most definite tendencies of his philosophy is precisely the condemnation of man and a series of demands addressed to him. Man, to Nietzsche, is a "being with perverted instincts," a "failed creature," one we cannot be content with. The entire task of the philosopher consists in "recreating" the human type. The "revaluation of all values" is nothing less than a demand for man to become different – to reject precisely those values that until now have defined the entire direction of his life.

Moreover, the philosopher of the future is called not only to recreate individuals but to change the entire direction of history.[113] And this change must take place in the sense of returning man to nature. Criticizing Rousseau, Nietzsche says in passing: "I also speak of a return to nature, although this is, strictly speaking, not a backward movement, but an ascent to free, even terrifying nature and naturalness-to that naturalness which plays with great tasks, dares to play with them."[114] Nature, with its indifference to good and evil, is now no longer presented as something identical to man, but as something above him – as an ideal that can be attained only by a few (Nietzsche sees Napoleon as a classic example of man's return to nature in the desired sense).

Consistent immoralism is first and foremost the rejection of all "ought" and of all ideals. And indeed, Nietzsche repeatedly speaks in this manner. Duty, he teaches, can only be discussed on the assumption of a universally recognized goal shared by humanity, but such a goal does not exist. It is true, one may recommend a goal to humanity – but in that case, the goal is not binding: everyone may choose to follow it or not, at their own discretion.[115]

And yet, from the same Nietzsche we learn that immoralists are also "men of duty," that they too have sacred obligations from which they cannot escape – for example, the obligation to love truth and to maintain unrelenting hostility against outdated views.[116] All of Nietzsche's teaching on values is a continuous oscillation between the recognition and the denial of objective moral norms, independent of human will.

Two opposing theses clash in this teaching. The first asserts that there are no values in nature at all. Every value presupposes some kind of goal, and since there are no goals in nature, and therefore no standard by which to evaluate what exists, there are no values in it either: our notion of "value" is a distortion of thought – a purely human invention and illusion, something that man brings into life.[117]

The opposing thesis, however, states that there are objective values in life, and that man must rid himself of his subjective illusions in order to accept the values given by nature itself.

In this contradiction lies the fundamental flaw of Nietzsche's entire attempt to justify life. If our judgments about the value or worthlessness of life were a matter of personal taste, of subjective arbitrariness, then the very attempt to justify life would be unnecessary and absurd. To justify life means to defend it with arguments that are convincing not just for me, but for others as well: it means to discover in it values that are not dependent on whim, but have objective significance, appear desirable for everyone, not just for me. And Nietzsche truly does find in the world something that appears to him objectively valuable: the force of life, endlessly renewing itself and triumphing over death, the grandeur and beauty of external nature.

But philosophical analysis immediately exposes the illusory nature of these values. If there are no goals in nature, then value, just like the beauty of nature, is an optical illusion, something that exists only for the imperfect eye of the observer. And again, we hear from Nietzsche that life in itself is unbearable, that only "the lie of art" can make it tolerable, that one must be a poet to invent consolation for oneself.[118]

Does this mean, then, that the "new tablets of values" by which Nietzsche wants to justify life are nothing more than seductive lies? But if so, why should they be preferred over the old tablets that Nietzsche wants to smash? After all, they, too, are seductive; traditional beliefs also adorn life! "We have painted things with new colors," says Nietzsche, "and we continue our painting incessantly; but what is our art compared to the splendor of the old master's colors – I mean, old humanity?"[119] Nietzsche rebels against the Christian justification of life because he sees in it a lie and because his love of truth refuses to accept what he considers a seductive deception. But what does Nietzsche offer in return for what he rejects? A justification of life that rests on "the lie of art"!

But we must ask: can we find peace in a conscious lie? Can the beauty of the universe bring us joy if we are aware that all this beauty is a complete illusion of our perception? We are offered solace in a world of beautiful dreams, but such solace seems impossible: beauty can bring us joy only as long as we believe in its objective reality; the moment we become aware that it is only a dream, we are freed from its enchantment. And the disappointment of ultimate awakening will be all the more terrible the more beautiful the dream was: the more seductive the vanishing mirage, the more painful the desert becomes for the traveler.

To Nietzsche's credit, it must be said that he was always above his own doctrine and never found complete satisfaction in it. After all he said about the value and joy of life, is it not strange to hear him confess: "The thought of suicide is a great consolation: with it many a dark night is successfully concluded."[120] Here we have a kind of "consolation" that at once destroys all the other consolations of Nietzsche's philosophy. Moreover, perhaps none of those consolations remain unexposed and unmocked by the author of *Zarathustra* himself. Let us listen, for example, to what he says about the beauty of the universe: "Man thinks that the universe itself is full of beauty, but he forgets himself as the cause of that beauty! He alone has bestowed beauty upon it – alas! Beauty that is human, all-too-human; in essence, man is admiring his own reflection in things: he finds beautiful everything that reflects his image; in judgments about beauty there is expressed the vanity of the human race."[121] It is hard to imagine a more complete discrediting of that very beauty in which Nietzsche sees the justification of human existence!

We have seen that for our philosopher, the highest thing man can attain is a "tragic disposition," which is expressed in "love of fate".[122] This love is shown in man's willingness to embrace the universe, to utter his "amen" to the fated sequence of its events.

Most interesting is that this very "tragic disposition" is again exposed and mocked by Nietzsche himself. "We laugh," he says, "at the man who, upon stepping outside during sunrise, says: 'I want the sun to rise.' We also laugh at the one who, unable to stop a turning wheel, says: 'I want it to turn.' And we laugh at the one who, thrown to the ground in a fight, says: 'Here I lie, for I want to lie here.' But jokes aside! Do we ever act any differently than these three when we utter our 'I will'?"[123]

This short aphorism contains a biting mockery of Nietzsche's own philosophy: here, all his "justification of life" is exposed as the expression of a comical impotence.

For Nietzsche, philosophy is above all an experiment upon his own life. He feels that his thought undermines the fundamental assumptions of his existence and asks himself: Is it possible to live with the truth?[124] We know that this experiment ended in Nietzsche's madness. And it could hardly have ended otherwise. He poured his entire soul into a doctrine that denies the purpose of life.

But this means denying precisely that which underlies our entire life and consciousness: every one of our desires, every movement of our thought is directed toward a goal, and every goal presupposes an ultimate goal – the basis and justification of all willing. Nietzsche rejects the absolute, rejects the final purpose, seeing in it the "shadow of God."

And yet, what is his philosophy if not a search for purpose? He remains religious even in his atheism: the "shadow of God" follows him at every step and gives him no peace.

CHAPTER: X

The Evaluation of Human Reason

The revaluation of all values in Nietzsche's philosophy is expressed, above all, in a new evaluation of human reason. As we turn to this section of his philosophy, we feel the ground beginning to shift beneath our feet. A whole labyrinth of contradictions opens before us. Here, confidence in reason and its extreme self-assertion suddenly give way to skepticism and despair. On one hand, Nietzsche is filled with joyful awareness of the power of human thought; on the other hand, for him, unreliability seems to be the very hallmark of all our intellectual activity. In human life, reason is the most valuable and at the same time the most valueless, the most contemptible thing: it is the source of our highest joys, and also our punishment – a kind of curse upon our existence; it is the goal of our life and at the same time its fiercest enemy.

Nietzsche sees the logical consequence of the atheist point of view in the idea that above our human wisdom, there is no other, higher wisdom.[125] Our human reason is the highest criterion of truth, goodness, and beauty: what should be recognized as valid is only what can be logically justified; every blind human belief not tested by reason deserves contempt as a result of intellectual dishonesty[126] and is doomed to perish, for there is no belief that can withstand the all-destroying force of logical analysis.

In Nietzsche's eyes, our reason, having killed God, thereby declares itself the highest force, subject to no one and absolutely free. The awareness of this power brings the philosopher cheerfulness and happiness: "For us, philosophers and free spirits," he says, "the news of the death of God is like the glimmer of a new dawn; our hearts overflow with gratitude, wonder, anticipation, and hope. At last, the horizon is open to us again – though perhaps not entirely clear; at last, our ships can set out again, heading for any danger; every daring act of knowledge is once more allowed! The sea is open again before us – our sea! Perhaps such a sea has never existed before."[127]

This mood is typified in the titles of two of Nietzsche's works – *Dawn* and *The Gay Science*. In his view, the joys of free thought bring new value to life. "No," he says, "life has not disappointed me. Year by year, it appears richer, more desirable, more mysterious – ever since the day when the great liberator came to me: the thought that life could be an experiment for the seeker, not a duty, a fatal accident, or a deception. Life is a means to knowledge"; "with this faith in our hearts, we can live not only courageously, but joyfully – even joyfully laugh".[128]

Free thought, however, does not necessarily bring happiness, for it awakens man from slumber and robs him of the peace that is a necessary condition for happiness. But it is the highest treasure, in comparison with which happiness itself fades. Why do we fear humanity's possible return to barbarism? Is it because barbarism brings unhappiness? No, the barbarians of all ages have been happier than we are. "But our drive for knowledge is too strong for us to value happiness without knowledge, or to be content with the happiness of constant self-deception." The will to know has become our dominant passion, and nothing can make us renounce it – even if we realize that it makes us miserable in our love for it.[129]

But on this path of self-assertion, Nietzsche's reason faces new disappointments. As soon as he attempts to realize the rights of free thought, philosophical analysis immediately reveals that there is no place for human reason in the structure of the universe. Confidence and pride vanish like smoke, replaced by a sense of powerlessness and insignificance.

Indeed, what can our human reason be in the midst of a

meaningless universe? Just a part of universal senselessness, of universal irrationality? But can one even speak of irrational reason? Would it not be a contradiction to say that our reason is meaningless in its fundamental drive and origin? Would this not simply mean admitting that it is something illusory – something only seeming? Or perhaps reason, in relation to the universe, is an exception – something alien to the whole? But that would contradict Nietzsche's basic premise: namely, that reason is not something special or exceptional in the world, but only a partial manifestation of the general order – or, more accurately, the general disorder – of the cosmos.

By the very formulation of this question, Nietzsche's thought is doomed to endless wandering: he continually vacillates between two diametrically opposed evaluations of human reason. His Zarathustra sees human wisdom as a kind of cosmic joke. "In all existence," he says, "one thing appears impossible – reason. It is true, a little reason is scattered among the stars, some seed of wisdom – this leaven is mixed into all things: wisdom is mixed into all things for the sake of folly."[130]

Consciousness, reason – they are nothing more than the privilege of a puny variety of the organic world – humanity. In relation to the world process as a whole, all of humanity's collective work is insignificant; even in relation to human life itself, the sphere of the conscious and rational is tiny: consciousness is just one of the functions of our organism, one means of its development, of increasing its overall power; thus, to regard consciousness or any sphere of the conscious as the highest value is exceedingly naive: it is to elevate a means to the status of an end, to deify one of the tools of our insignificant existence.[131]

Human life, like all that exists, is illogical at its root, irrational in its very essence: if our consciousness is nothing more than an instrument of this life, then it too is illogical in its original source. The entire domain of logic originally emerged from the illogical; our reason is the product and culmination of instincts aimed at preserving our organism and increasing its power. Can we be sure that our developed consciousness has lost the stamp of its origins, that it has gradually become logical? Nietzsche answers this in the negative: our reason now, as before, remains the servant of our blind instincts. "The process of logical thought and reasoning in our current brain corresponds to the development and struggle of drives, each of which is highly illogical and untruthful; usually we become aware only of the outcome of this struggle – so quickly and secretly does this ancient mechanism work within us."[132] The illogical in man is necessary; this is one of those discoveries capable of driving the thinker to despair.[133]

If that is so, then we must ask: is our reason suited to the knowledge of truth – does it deserve our trust at all? Evidently, it does not. Since the function of reason is merely to serve as a tool for the preservation of the human species, all our thinking appears to be absolutely unreliable: some truths are fatal for us; many illusions are necessary for our survival and power. Therefore, in order to fulfill its function, reason must remain a realm of illusions – illusions that are beneficial for humanity. "In the end," asks Nietzsche, "what are human truths? They are his irrefutable errors."[134]

I call the reader's attention to the fact that these opposing evaluations of human reason cannot be attributed to different periods of Nietzsche's work, as they appear side by side in the very same writings. The famous text on life as a means to knowledge appears in the same book, *Die fröhliche Wissenschaft*, where reason is described as a tool of illogical, blind instincts.

Through critical analysis, Nietzsche seeks to uncover the falsehoods underlying our consciousness. One such assumption is our belief in truth. Truth is understood as that which is necessary and constant in things: that which cannot be otherwise. The impressions on which we base our judgments about the external world and ourselves are ever-changing; yet we assume that behind this ceaseless change lies something fixed, something that constitutes the actual being of things, their enduring truth.

But in this assumption lies the first and fundamental lie of our consciousness, for everything in the world is in flux and nothing remains unchanged. To assume that there is something permanent in the world is to assume a halt, a break in the flow; meanwhile, the essential property of the world process is precisely its continuity, and thus, the absence of anything permanent or abiding.

All our knowledge amounts to searching for the constant properties of things – that is, precisely what does not exist in them. This false belief in the constancy of existence is rooted, like all the other prejudices of our reason, in physiological needs, in our organism's inherent drive for self-preservation and growth.

If we didn't believe, for example, that fire always burns, that certain animals are always helpful and others always harmful, our species would have long perished. Our constancy in belief saves us – and so we take this constancy to be a property of things themselves.

The entire process of our cognition is thus: we elevate the conditions of our survival to the status of objective properties of the universe.[135]

"What are the categories of our reason and our logical laws? They are representations that proved useful in the process of human evolution for the preservation of the species. Because of their usefulness, they became objects of fixed belief and acquired for us the status of unshakable and a priori truths. In other words, our cognitive process rests on the assumption that what is useful to us is what is true."[136]

Can we at least believe in the constancy of our logical laws – in their unchanging nature as forms of our consciousness? From Nietzsche's point of view, this is impermissible. The very forms of our consciousness are something that has arisen in time: they belong to the kind of human being we know – that is, the human as he has existed for the last four millennia. This gives us no right to speak of their eternity.

In the realm of human consciousness, as in all that exists, there are no eternal facts, no absolute truths.[137] In all human judgments, man himself – his utility, his desire to dominate things – serves as the criterion. But since man is constantly changing, he cannot have a stable standard for judging things; thus, our judgments express not truth, but merely our passing moods. From this standpoint, Nietzsche says, we ought, strictly speaking, to abandon all judgment altogether – but we are incapable of this: man is so constituted that he inevitably feels attraction to some things and aversion to others; he cannot live without valuing things, and therefore – without judging them.[138]

Faith in reason is connected with a critical attitude toward the evidence of our senses: metaphysics in every age has opposed reason, as the realm of certainty and truth, to deceptive sense-perception. However different metaphysical systems may be, they have always agreed that authentic being is supersensible; everything accessible to the senses, by contrast, belongs to the domain of illusory, apparent being.

Nietzsche takes precisely the opposite view: he connects the rejection of reason with a rehabilitation of the senses – and with mockery of all metaphysics. For him, only the sensually perceived world, with all its endless variety and changeability, is true and real.

Among the ancients, the Eleatics doubted the trustworthiness of our senses because the senses show us diversity and change, while actual being, they claimed, is one and unchanging. Heraclitus, on the other hand, thought our senses deceive us by showing us constancy and unity, which are actually not present. Nietzsche, who holds Heraclitus in the highest regard for his view of being as a continuous process, nevertheless believes Heraclitus was also wrong in his skepticism toward the senses.

Our senses, Nietzsche argues, do not lie – neither in the sense of the Eleatics, nor in that of Heraclitus. Our reason is the one that falsifies the testimony of the senses, introducing into them false concepts such as unity, permanence, substance, and so on.

To the extent that our senses testify to constant flux, change, and destruction, they do not lie. Only our reason lies – insofar as it asserts that beyond our senses there exists a true world, one that is supersensible and eternal.[139]

The essence of Nietzsche's thought is that the world accessible to our senses is the only reality; the supersensible is, in his view, a remnant of the divine – the "shadow of God". Metaphysics, which preaches the existence of an actual world beyond appearances, is a vestige of theology, a feeble attempt to replace religion.

To be entirely freed from religion, one must also overcome metaphysics. It is not enough to point out the shortcomings of individual systems: one must root out the religious need that underlies all religious and metaphysical doctrines.[140]

In his struggle against metaphysics, Nietzsche clearly realizes that metaphysical assumptions – or, in other words, representations of the supersensible – underlie all our judgments. At the foundation of all metaphysics lies the opposition between the truly real and the merely apparent, between the world as it is in itself and the world as it appears to us – between the thing-in-itself and phenomena. By rejecting the supersensible, Nietzsche wants nothing to do with any metaphysical "essences." Our concepts of "substance" and "thing-in-itself," in his view, deserve Homeric laughter.[141]

If that is so, one must ask: can we still speak of phenomena from this perspective? To regard the world accessible to our senses as the realm of phenomena is to admit that beneath this world lies some essence which is revealed to us. Every phenomenon is the phenomenon *of* something real – in other words, the manifestation of some essence. Whoever rejects essence, or equivalently the "thing in itself," must then reject phenomena, too. That is precisely what Nietzsche does: if there is no thing in itself, he says, then there is no "phenomenon."[142] If there is no world "truly existing," then there is also no "apparent world."[143] There are, in fact, no "things" at all; for the very concept of "thing" rests on the false assumption of something abiding, unmoving, which is not given to our senses; and even the concept of "being" is false, since it rests on that same fiction. Truly existent is only eternal becoming, an uninterrupted process.[144]

Here arises the question: is it becoming possible without something that becomes? Every process, every motion presupposes something mobile – that which becomes: apparently, the concept of process presupposes the concept of essence, the concept of a subject which undergoes the process, relative to which "process" is a predicate. From Nietzsche's viewpoint, however, this is nothing but prejudice. Just because we cannot conceive a predicate without a subject does not mean that beneath the cosmic process lies a real subject or essence. Our grammatical laws are not the laws of the universe. The very concept of subject is our invention, our fiction, through which we think the existing.

Step by step, Nietzsche arrives at the conclusion that our "I" is a fiction. Descartes taught: "I think, therefore I am." In these words, Nietzsche argues, is expressed the inference from the fact of thought to the existence of a real subject or essence that thinks. In that, inference is merely shown by our grammatical habit of attributing every action to an agent. In truth, from the fact of thought we are not entitled to conclude to the reality of our "I," or even of any "something" that thinks.[145]

On the same grounds, Nietzsche rejects the notion of causality. This concept, in his view, is rooted in that same grammatical prejudice: from every event we immediately infer an agent who produces it. That presumed agent, to whom we ascribe the occurrence, is what we call "cause." In truth, "causality" is only our subjective fiction: there are no essences, no "agents," and therefore no causes or actions; the world process cannot be dissected into causes and effects, because it does not decompose into distinct points – it flows continuously.[146] A causal explanation of the universe is essentially an attempt to interpret it by analogy with what we observe in our inner world: seeing our muscles move after a specific act of will, we imagine our will to be the agent, the cause. Applying that analogy outward, we conclude that behind every external event lies a cause, a driving agent, just as our will drives our motions. But this chain of inference is false. Internally, we do not directly observe the will as a subject or agent: instead, we see only a sequence or succession of states. We observe that after a volition comes motion, and we wrongly infer from this a metaphysical subject, our will, that produces both. The further error is to interpret the external world by internal analogy. That is an arbitrary attempt to humanize nature.[147]

Our consciousness is, in general, a continuous realm of fictions. Our logical axioms are as illusory as the categories of our understanding. For example, the famous "law of contradiction" is purely a subjective rule of our thought, for which we have no right to assign objective status. From the fact that we cannot both affirm and deny the same thing does not follow that what cannot possess contradictory properties. The law of contradiction is not a property of what exists; it is an expression of our human limitation. We do not know being; therefore, we cannot decide whether our logical axioms apply to it or not. Thus, they are not criteria of truth, but prescriptions about what should be counted as true.[148]

One may ask: under such conditions, can we speak at all of knowledge? Nietzsche explicitly states that we can rather *establish* our attitudes to things, not *know* them: even the most precise methods of scientific inquiry cannot give us more.[149] But we do not need more: what if truth is inaccessible to us! Believing that truth is more valuable than falsehood is itself one of the greatest prejudices. Illusions often most effectively further the preservation of the human species; conversely, many "truths" may turn out to be fatal to us. Therefore, the falsity of some judgment is no sufficient objection to it: the question is, to what extent can it aid the preservation and growth of our life.[150] Consistent with this, Nietzsche holds that the aim of philosophy through the ages has not been truth, but health – that is, the increase of our power.[151]

CHAPTER: XI

To anyone familiar with the history of philosophy, the entire series of opposing theses just outlined presents nothing new. As early as antiquity, a conclusion was drawn from Heraclitus' teaching that if there is nothing permanent or constant in the world, then there is nothing true: on that basis, even Heraclitus' disciple Cratylus arrived at the conviction that every human judgment is false. Finally, in the Sophists, we find – in connection with elements of Heraclitus' doctrine – the same positions: denial of truth, denial of "being," denial of the possibility of knowledge, as well as the communicability of our concepts through language, and ultimately the same subordination of theory to practical needs; associated with this is the assertion that the aim of our judgments is not truth but the increase of our power.

As has been said, Nietzsche fully recognizes his kinship with both Heraclitus and the Sophists: "Our present way of thinking," he says, "is highly Heraclitean, Democritean, and Protagorean; it is enough to call it Protagorean, since Protagoras united in himself both Heraclitus and Democritus."[152] Nietzsche's sympathy for the Sophists is reinforced by the fact that he sees in them not only forerunners of a true theory of knowledge, but also the first immoralists of antiquity – precursors of his own moral philosophy.[153] The teaching of the Sophists, overall, represents for him the highest point of Greek philosophical development: after them begins the period of decline.[154]

It is clear that skepticism, taken to such an extreme, cannot remain consistent. Every logical denial is an active assertion of our reason and, to that extent, an affirmation of reason itself. When our reason and logic – that which does the denying – become the object of denial, we fall into an evident contradiction. Our doubt in thought is belied by the very act of thinking that doubts. If every judgment is false, then the skeptic's own judgment – denying the possibility of knowledge – is also false. Absolute doubt must ultimately negate itself – or, in other words, become affirmation.

In Nietzsche's teaching, we have already seen this combination of opposing extremes – the denial of reason and belief in it. This is tied to his contradictory attitude toward philosophy itself. He rebels against every form of dogmatism, seeing in all dogmas – religious or philosophical – expressions of intellectual childhood.[155] Yet in his own philosophy, we find numerous dogmas. He declares the unknowability of being; the very concept of "true being" is for him an illusion – and yet, we find in his work a series of positive assertions about being. He proclaims himself an enemy of all metaphysics; and yet, it is not difficult to demonstrate that his system contains numerous metaphysical constructions – and relatively poor ones at that.

First, being is defined by Nietzsche in terms of negative propositions: it is meaningless, purposeless, devoid of reason. In addition, he provides it with a set of positive definitions: it is an uninterrupted process. In the mouth of a thinker who denies the possibility of eternal truths, it sounds especially strange to hear an affirmation of the eternity of cosmic motion, of the eternal recurrence of life. Delving deeper into his thought, we see that for Nietzsche, not only is the process itself eternal – something abides at its core and persists through all transformations of the universe: this is world energy, which, according to Nietzsche, neither increases nor diminishes, but remains eternally the same. The doctrine of the eternal recurrence of all things – one of the cornerstones of Nietzsche's philosophy – is derived, as we saw, from the law of the constancy or eternity of world energy. While denying causality, he simultaneously attempts to reduce the world process to its primal, eternal cause. The initial cause of all cosmic development, he claims, itself does not undergo development and does not arise in time.[156]

In this distinction between the realm of the transitory and changing, on the one hand, and the eternal foundation of the universe on the other, we recognize the very opposition of phenomenon and thing-in-itself that Nietzsche himself declared worthy of Homeric laughter. Having rejected this dichotomy, he nevertheless continues to speak as if nothing has happened, discussing the "phenomenal" side of the cosmos and opposing it to the "non-phenomenal." According to his definition, being is "will to power." Every atom of matter is endowed with a tendency to assert itself in space, to occupy a position by pushing out all other particles; every human being and every living creature is driven not only to preserve, but to expand its being, to attain the most significant possible surplus of energy. All that exists strives for power. The will to power is "the innermost essence of being" (das innerste Wesen des Seins). All else is phenomenal: phenomenal are our representations of "subjects," "things," and the like. Only the primal source of all world phenomena is "non-phenomenal".[157] Once again, we are dealing with unconscious metaphysics; these cited passages are taken from the same posthumous work in which Nietzsche rejects the dichotomy of thing-in-itself and appearance,[158] and where he elaborates at length on the impossibility of knowledge.

We saw that Nietzsche considers the senses to be the "only reliable domain," and regards belief in the suprasensory as a symptom of decline. And yet, his metaphysics thrusts us entirely into the realm of the suprasensory. Inaccessible to the senses is the world energy that gives rise to all things; likewise, inaccessible is the eternity of being – the infinite time over which the world process unfolds – for the senses can perceive only the limited, the transient, the finite. Nietzsche's philosophy might appear to be complete sensualism, and yet we find him somewhere speaking against sensualism as a vulgar worldview, warning against boundless trust in the senses; here he declares that our senses deceive us, that true being does not coincide with the vi-sible and tangible, and he even expresses a certain sympathy for Plato's philosophy, which, in all respects, was an aristocratic reaction against the vulgar cult of the tangible.[159]

In a word, Nietzsche's entire philosophy is conditioned by the application to being of the very categories of reason that he seeks to deny; his doctrine of knowledge is a continuous struggle between two mutually exclusive tendencies. To fully understand this doctrine, it is not enough to uncover its contradictions; we must also explain how and why these contradictions arise.

First of all, as already stated, the denial of human reason is a necessary logical consequence of Nietzsche's fundamental principles. A philosophy that denies the existence of any universal purposes at the foundation of the cosmos must, understandably, deny the suitability of human reason for the universal goal of discovering truth. Faith in human reason already presupposes an objective teleology – precisely what Nietzsche rejects.

Furthermore, knowledge is possible only if being can be expressed in concepts of reason. If being is something absolutely opposed to and alien from thought, then it cannot be expressed in the terms of thought and cannot be known or understood by us. Every act of cognition presupposes that the concepts in which it is expressed are not mere subjective illusions, but have objective and universal significance – are the forms of reality itself, the forms of actual phenomena of being. In other words, knowledge presupposes that thought lies at the foundation of existence, expresses its very nature: otherwise, what exists would not conform to the forms of thought and would be entirely unknowable.

Our human knowledge is only possible on the assumption of a universal, all-encompassing reason. This assumption underlies all our judgments – whether or not these judgments intend to be metaphysical, and whether they relate to being or to its phenomena. When Kant said that the forms of consciousness underlie the world of phenomena as conditions of its possibility, he stopped halfway. There is no phenomenon without the essence that appears; therefore, if we say that thought is a universal and necessary form of phenomena, we are inevitably led to conclude that thought is the universal predicate – the universal determination of being.

Thus, the dilemma arises: either a universal thought exists, encompassing all that is, or knowledge is altogether impossible. Nietzsche chose the second horn of the dilemma: having denied the existence of universal thought at the basis of reality, he had to accept the necessary consequence – that every human judgment is false.

Nietzsche understood that belief in human reason rests upon the metaphysical presupposition of a reason higher than man. Wishing to be consistent, he renounced both. His example is instructive in another respect: it proves that within us lies an ineradicable, albeit unconscious, metaphysical faith that mocks our denials. The denial of reason, the denial of the very possibility of judgment, remains nonetheless a judgment; like every other rational act, it presupposes faith in reason – that very thing which it seeks to negate.

CHAPTER: XII

Critique of Contemporary Morality

That which has been laid out above sufficiently prepares us for understanding that part of Nietzsche's doctrine which he himself considered the most important – namely, the teaching about man and his practical task. "In every philosophy," he says, "moral or immoral intentions constitute the life-seed from which the whole plant grows." Philosophy is never the product of a purely theoretical interest: it is determined by the struggle of manifold practical drives within the philosopher's soul, by the totality of those life-demands which this struggle evokes. Hence, the center of gravity of every philosophy lies in its morality, in its ethics.[160]

With respect to Nietzsche's own philosophy, this is no less true. All his arguments about God, the world, religion, metaphysics, and the theory of knowledge are attempts to disentangle human values. Judgment upon man is the fundamental task of his thinking.

From Nietzsche's standpoint, this judgment is not a moral evaluation, for as we have already seen, his philosophy aims first and foremost at immoralism, i.e., the total negation of morality. One can speak of moral duty – universal and unconditional – only by assuming an objective goal underlying the development of the universe and of humanity. Since no such goal exists, what sense can moral standards have? "At present," Nietzsche says, "we everywhere hear roughly the following definition of the purpose of morality: it is to preserve humanity and move it forward; but to speak thus is simply to rest on formulas, for immediately arises the question: Preserve in what sense? Move forward to where? Has the essence – the answer to those questions – been omitted from the formula? Can we, by means of that formula, derive anything in the doctrine of duties that is not already surreptitiously assumed, unaccounted for? Can we see from it clearly whether we ought to strive for the longest possible duration of human life or for the greatest possible transcendence of animality? The means – i.e., practical morality – would differ greatly in the two cases. Suppose we wish to impart to humanity the highest possible rationality: this would not, of course, guarantee the longest possible duration. Or suppose that "the highest happiness" of humanity is our final end! But what do we understand by that – the highest degree of happiness that certain individuals might gradually reach, or a maximal average happiness of all, which defies computation? And why should morality bring that? For through morality a host of sources of discontent have been opened; one might rather think that every improvement of morality so far has made man less content with himself, his neighbor, and his fate in life! Have not the most moral people so far thought that deep suffering is the only condition of man that can be justified from a moral standpoint?[161]

In the absence of an unconditional goal for humanity, it is absurd to speak of duty, to address any moral demands to people.[162] There are no prescriptions that can have universal validity.[163] Since there is no universal goal, there can be no universal legislation, no single path for all people. "This is my path," says Zarathustra, "and where is your path?" he responded to those asking him about the path. "The path you ask about does not exist at all."[164]

Under these conditions, there can be no talk of moral facts. "A moral judgment," Nietzsche says, "converges with a religious judgment in that both believe in non-existent realities. Morality is merely an interpretation of certain phenomena – more precisely, a false interpretation. A moral judgment, like a religious one, belongs to that stage of ignorance in which the very concept of the real is absent, the very distinction between the actual and the imaginary; so that at that stage the word 'truth' denotes only what we now call 'fancies.'[165] Our moral intentions rest on error, and thus that traditional morality which judges human actions by their intentions is as much a prejudice as astrology or alchemy.[166]

For Nietzsche, the fundamental error of many modern moral theories lies in the fact that, having rejected Christianity, they believe they can retain Christian morality. But they cannot. "By rejecting Christian faith, we thereby deprive ourselves of the right to Christian morality." "Christianity is a system, a considered and integral worldview. If we discard its fundamental notion – the notion of God – we thereby destroy the whole: nothing necessary remains in hand."[167]

This remark constitutes the guiding thread of all of Nietzsche's critical work in ethics. Step by step dismantling the basic concepts of contemporary morality, he argues that in an age that has outgrown religious belief, those concepts cannot stand.

"Critique of contemporary morality" for him is above all a critique of altruism. Today, a person is deemed moral if in all his actions he is guided by sympathetic impulses, compassion, and selfless love for others. Despite the differences in their justifications of morality, most modern moralists roughly agree in the content of its demands: nearly all agree that the individual must deny himself, live for others, and for society as a whole. From this vantage, the individual's happiness is seen to lie in his best adjustment to social needs – to serve as an instrument of common well-being, as though the moral task is precisely to deprive personality of all autonomy.[168]

Nietzsche's worldview was initially shaped under the influence of Schopenhauer, the most eloquent among modern preachers of compassion. Once he overcame that influence, his rebellion against altruistic morality was expressed mainly in polemics against Schopenhauer's ethical teaching. Madame Lou

Andréas Salomé[169] finds that the middle period of Nietzsche's writing, in contrast to the later, is characterized by sympathy for the morality of compassion and praise of benevolent impulses. Yet Nietzsche himself, in one of his later writings, says that it was precisely in that period that the polemic against the morality of compassion and the dismantling of altruism in general was his most important task. The evidence is the quotations he gives from *Menschliches* and *Morgenröthe*.[170]

According to Schopenhauer, the essence of compassion consists in the self-forgetting of the individual. In compassion, we identify ourselves with another suffering being; therefore, compassion is, as it were, an act of insight into the unity of all that exists. By feeling the suffering of another as our own, we thereby detach ourselves from the boundaries of our individuality, cease to live a personal life: we feel that the single world-substance, the single will in all beings, suffers and is tormented.

Nietzsche, through a number of arguments, demonstrates the untenability of this psychological analysis of compassion. In compassion, the self is never forgotten. Between what we feel upon witnessing suffering and what the suffering person themselves experiences, there is neither identity nor even similarity. "The suffering of another offends us; it would reveal us to ourselves as weak, perhaps even as cowardly, if we did not come to their aid. Sometimes it entails a diminishment of our own honor in our eyes or in the eyes of others. At times, in another's misfortune and suffering lies a reminder of danger that threatens us; and already as evidence of the precariousness and insecurity of human life in general, it can act upon us in an oppressive way. By ridding ourselves of such burdensome and offensive feelings, we repay them with an act of compassion; in it lies a subtle self-defense or even revenge."[171]

In short, in the act of compassion, we strive to rid ourselves of our own suffering, which has nothing to do with the suffering of the other. Finally, to the act of compassion, there is sometimes added our own pleasure. Firstly, a strong emotion is in itself a source of enjoyment – this is evident, for example, in the impression made upon us by tragedy; and finally, the very act of helping another can serve as a source of diverse pleasures for us, whether because it releases accumulated excess energy, or because it flatters our vanity or dispels our boredom. That in compassion we do not forget ourselves, but rather think intensely about ourselves, is proven, among other things, by the following: in many cases we could simply turn away from another's suffering, withdraw from it; if we do not do this, but instead rush to aid the sufferer, we thereby show that we are mindful of ourselves, that we are asserting ourselves.

If, in compassion, a person truly renounced everything personal, everything individual, they would be elevated to a complete understanding of another's suffering. But in fact, quite the opposite occurs: in the vast majority of cases, compassion reveals a crude misunderstanding. The most profound, most personal of our sufferings usually remain incomprehensible and inaccessible to others. When our suffering is noticed by others, it is usually interpreted in the most superficial manner; "the essential feature of the compassionate emotion lies precisely in that it strips the suffering of the other of all that is personal, all that is particular." Hence, the offensiveness of benefactions. Benefactors who do not understand the source of our suffering offend and humiliate our dignity more than enemies do.[172]

If, then, compassion is not a penetration into the suffering of another, it is simply a duplication of suffering.[173] When we elevate compassion to the fundamental principle of our morality, we thereby turn it into an effect destructive to life. Insofar as compassion is truly a source of suffering, it is harmful like any weakness; the benefit it brings in individual cases cannot justify it, for overall it increases suffering in the world. If for even one day it were to become the ruling feeling, humanity would immediately perish. Let us indeed imagine what would become of us if the following rule prevailed in life: "Feel the sufferings of your neighbor as he himself feels them." If this rule became reality for us, if we really could continuously feel the full weight of not only our own but every other person's suffering, then we would not be able to endure life even for the shortest time.[174]

In contrast to those tonic affects that elevate vital energy, compassion acts oppressively on our sense of well-being. Suffering is already in itself associated with a loss of vital force; compassion entails a new and significant increase in this loss. It is understandable, then, that the preaching of compassion is linked to Schopenhauer's pessimistic doctrine: compassion is the denial of life; it portrays life as worthy of denial; it convinces us to strive for its annihilation. However, universal annihilation is rarely elevated to a principle with complete frankness: usually it is masked by words such as "God," "true life," "nirvana," "salvation," "bliss." According to Nietzsche, the ordinary meaning of all these consoling words of religion and morality is condemnation, denial of life, and the root of this life-hostile orientation lies in compassion.

By multiplying suffering in the world, compassion also increases the very number of sufferers: in general, it paralyzes the operation of the fundamental law of development – the law of natural selection. It preserves all that is already ready to perish: it postpones the end of the destitute and those condemned by life; by artificially sustaining the existence of all sorts of failures, it thereby gives life a more gloomy and dubious aspect.[175]

The very fact of compassion is evidence of decline, of a weakening of vital energy. The debilitated, degenerate man of our time is unable to stand on his own feet, finds it immensely difficult to support his own existence, and thus he requires the "compassion" of his neighbor. We all help each other; each of us has become, to some extent, a patient and at the same time a nurse at the bedside of the sick. And this is called "virtue"! Among people who have known life otherwise – abundantly, fully, extravagantly – this would be called something else: "cowardice," or perhaps "baseness," "womanish morality." The very softening of our mores is a consequence of decline. Conversely, the cruelty and danger of mores are a consequence of an excess of vital force. Strong epochs, noble cultures see in compassion, in "love of neighbor," in the absence of self-assertion and self-awareness, something contemptible. The very popularity of Schopenhauer's morality of "compassion" is proof of the degeneration of the human type characteristic of our era.[176]

CHAPTER: XIII

A sign of decay is not only the morality of compassion but any morality in general, since it always contains a residue of altruism. Morality always and everywhere expresses itself in one or another evaluation and thus in establishing a certain hierarchical order relative to human drives and actions. In these evaluations, the needs of each particular society manifest themselves: that which is useful to it in the first place, second, and third becomes the highest criterion for determining the value of each individual. Morality accustoms the individual to be a function of the herd and to value himself only in terms of that function. Since the conditions for preservation differ greatly among societies, there have been many different moralities; in view of future transformations of human societies, one can predict that many divergent moral viewpoints will continue to exist.[177]

Accordingly, our modern cult of altruism does not express an eternal moral principle, but a specific stage of development – that is, the condition of a distorted, corrupted society. In his judgments about man, Nietzsche wants to stand outside the moral point of view, and thus, for him, words such as "perversion," "decay," "corruption," etc., do not imply moral condemnation. "I call corrupted," he says, "any animal, race, or individual when it has lost its instincts, when it elects what is harmful to it." What is useful to any living being is the increase of power; what is harmful is its diminution; when an individual's drive toward power weakens, he is on the path to decay.[178]

From this point of view Nietzsche rises up against altruistic morality: it condemns in man precisely that striving which is the guarantee of his flourishing – his egoism, his self-love. Instead, it praises everything that injures his development. Thus, for example, we praise diligence, even though it spoils the eyes, damages the freshness and receptivity of the spirit; we honor the youth who overworks himself to his own detriment; we exalt actions and qualities which, being harmful to the individual, at the same time produce a type that appears beneficial to society; by public benefit we are ready to justify every sacrifice of the individual: we wish to cultivate in him the temperament of a sacrificial animal. On the contrary, we look with horror on every person who desires to live for himself, who places his preservation and development above serving society.[179] Likewise, in works usually attributed to Nietzsche's middle period, in that text, the doctrine which prefers social welfare over individual welfare is called "the philosophy of the sacrificial animal."[180]

One might ask: Does such a position follow from the principle of common utility, or is it necessary for the sake of preservation of the species? History informs us to the contrary: it shows that selfish drives have been the strongest motors of humanity. For humanity to grow and strengthen, evil is necessary – those dangers which temper the will, those strong passions without which man is unable to create anything great: lust for power, envy, greed, violence, malice – all these qualities are as necessary for the advancement of the human species as their opposites.[181] Gazing into the lives of the greatest people and the mightiest nations, we see that storms and hardships have been necessary for their growth in greatness and power.[182]

The strongest and "evil" people have always been the chief agents of humanity. They ignited dormant passions in society, awakened the spirit of comparison and conflict, the struggle of opinions and ideals, and the search for what is new and untested. They did so by raising arms, by overturning boundary stones, by insulting sacred things. The same "malice" that makes the conqueror loathed is also in each teacher, each preacher of the new, though there its manifestations are more subtle. The new is under any conditions "evil," for it is precisely that which seeks to conquer, to topple old boundaries and sacred things. The proven historical utility of evil is, to Nietzsche, a better refutation of modern utilitarian morality: the latter erroneously identifies the good with the expedient and beneficial, and the evil with the inexpedient and harmful.[183] In the end, morality is nothing but obedience to mores; conversely, evil is that which is unforeseeable, unusual.[184] Again, this anti-utilitarian standpoint appears in a work attributed to Nietzsche's "middle period." From this, it is clear that the suppression of evil would be equivalent to the perpetuation of the status quo – i.e., the end of all progressive movement. Great epochs of our life begin at the moment when we have the courage to recognize the evil as the best in us.[185] All greatness contains in itself crime; only what stands outside morality is great.[186]

Not only is evil beneficial, but suffering is also beneficial; this is the refutation of that hedonistic morality which places the aim of life in removing suffering and in achieving as large a sum of pleasures as possible. "You want, as far as possible, to eradicate suffering," says Nietzsche, "and how insane this 'as far as possible' is; but we, on the contrary, prefer that it be stronger and worse than ever before. Prosperity, as you understand it, is, from our point of view, not a goal but an end. It is a state that immediately makes a man ridiculous, worthy of contempt, and forces us to wish for its annihilation. The school of suffering – great suffering – do you not know that only this school has hitherto created every greatness of man? Ingenuity, endurance, courage, everything in our soul that is mysterious and profound, our intellect and cunning – all this is nurtured by suffering, misfortune, and dangers."[187]

From this arises the fundamental reproach that Nietzsche levels at modern morality: it belittles and diminishes man, hinders his growth, because its primary impulse is fear of anything that rises above the standard level of mediocrity. Herein lies the secret of the nowadays fashionable principle of "sympathy for one's neighbor"; the entire task of modern morality reduces to removing from life all danger that once belonged to it. From this viewpoint, only those actions aimed at public safety and social tranquillity are understood as "good." By eliminating all roughness and irregularity from life, we are on the path to turning humanity into sand – fine, round, soft, endless sand.[188]

If we dig into the conscience of the modern European, we find in every corner, in every fold of modern moral consciousness, the same imperious herd-fear: "We want that one day there will be nothing left to fear!" That aspiration is today called "progress." But there was a time when people thought differently. In the days when the foundations of human societies were laid, when people had to overcome many external dangers, fight against countless external enemies, the herd instinct led men to value more dangerous qualities of human nature, because in those times their usefulness to the herd was evident. In the times of the Roman Republic, for instance, virtues such as enterprise, bold courage, thirst for revenge, cunning, greed, and ambition were honoured rather than neighbor-love; of course, they were called by other names then, but still they were exalted and celebrated. When the foundations of human societies were strengthened and external danger weakened, fear of one's neighbor predominated over all and opened new horizons for moral evaluation. Then society perceived the danger of those very traits once held in esteem and began to brand them immoral. At the same time, the opposite traits became honored virtues: people began to revere whatever is mediocre and safe in human desires, ambitions, opinions, and even gifts. Now, any intellectual independence, any unwillingness to go with the crowd, even outstanding intellect, is felt as a danger. Henceforth, all that rises above the herd and causes fear in the neighbor is called evil; the "lambs and sheep" enjoy honor in modern society.[189] Modern European morality is nothing more and nothing less than "the morality of herding animals."[190] It has turned man from a wild animal into a "tame, domestic" one; thanks to it, the last traces of former greatness, the remnants of what man once was, vanish in our days.[191]

Today, "good" is deemed the one who does not violate, does not insult, does not attack another, does not take revenge, but entrusts vengeance to God, who hides, avoids confrontation with evil, and demands little of life. All the "meek, humble, righteous" act this way. Without prejudice, this means, in other words, "We are weak, and since we are weak, it is better not to do that for which we are not strong enough." But do insects not do exactly that when they pretend to be dead as danger approaches, so as not to overreach themselves? Such is the falsehood and deceit of weakness that it portrays itself as the virtue of voluntary humility and self-denial.[192] The tendency of all later civilizations, including our European one, is expressed in the proverb given to Chinese children from youth: "Make your heart small."[193]

In benevolent impulses, one sees, above all, the absorption of the individual by society. Speaking in physiological terms, this means one cell – the person – has become a function of a more powerful cell – society: the latter assimilates the former. To speak of good and evil, of virtue and vice, in that regard is wholly inappropriate, since we deal with an expression of natural necessity, which is subject not to moral judgment but to physiological explanation. One cell submits, another rules not because one is good and the other evil, but because both subordination and domination flow from their nature.[194] All our moral concepts and rules, all tablets of our values, have a physiological substrate which must be elucidated by science.[195]

CHAPTER: XIV

The Origin of Morality

The morality of physiologically strong races differs essentially from the morality of weak and degenerate races. This is the starting point of Nietzsche's doctrine of the origin of morality.

Ultimately, people are divided into predatory and domestic animals – eagles and lambs – rulers and the ruled. There are races destined by nature for domination: at the foundation of these aristocratic races, there always lies the predator, the "blond beast," which strives for victory and booty.[196] Other human races, on the contrary, by their inborn qualities must inevitably become prey. Corresponding to these two fundamental types of humankind are two types of morality – the morality of masters and the morality of slaves.

In mixed human societies, containing both aristocratic and democratic elements, moral notions often represent a blending of these opposite types. Nevertheless, these types remain original and fundamental. All moral evaluations arose either in the environment of rulers, filled with the consciousness of their superiority over inferiors, or in the environment of the ruled. In the first case – that is, when the concept of the good is established by masters – it designates everything that separates the higher from the lower, all those states of soul that elevate above the mass, establish distance, and institute hierarchical order among people. Here, aristocracy becomes synonymous with nobility, the mob with baseness. The opposition of "good and bad" is reduced to the opposition of "noble and despicable" – the base.

From the point of view of this master morality, everything considered a property of the "lower" is branded with contempt: cowardice, pettiness, narrow utilitarian calculation; an object of repulsion is the doglike servility with which the "lower" person accepts humiliation, flattery, and begging, and above all, falsehood. All aristocrats are convinced of the mendacity of ordinary people. "We are the truthful" – thus the aristocrats of ancient Greece called themselves. The original moral evaluations refer here not to actions, but to persons. All aristocratic morality is a glorification of a definite class of people – in other words, self-glorification. The aristocracy sees itself as the source of all good and all value; it recognizes as good only its equals; it considers evil everything that is evil for it. In all its disposition, there is manifest a sense of fullness, an overflow of power seeking to burst outward. To such an aristocratic conception of morality, compassion is alien; instead, there belongs to it a generosity conditioned by the surplus of wealth and might. The most typical and at the same time most alien trait of aristocratic morality to our age is that it recognizes obligations only toward equals: toward lower beings, it leaves open unlimited space for discretion and arbitrariness.

The second type of morality – the morality of slaves – is in everything opposed to the first. Let us imagine that lawgivers in the domain of morality are people oppressed, crushed, suffering, unfree, insecure in themselves, and weary. What will their moral evaluation be, corresponding to their condition? In all probability, it will express a pessimistic mood, disappointment in human life as a whole, condemnation of man and his position in the world. The slave judges unfavorably the virtue of the strong: he looks with mistrust at everything that in them is honored as good; he wants even to convince himself that they have no true happiness. On the contrary, he highly values all those qualities which ease the existence of the suffering: above all, compassion, the hand ready to help, a warm heart, patience, diligence, humility – all these are the most valuable qualities, without which life itself would be unbearable.

The morality of slaves is essentially the morality of utility.

Here for the first time arises the opposition of good and evil, which, strictly speaking, is foreign to aristocratic morality. Evil here is above all strength, everything dangerous and terrible, everything that does not allow itself to be despised. From the standpoint of slave morality, the "evil" man arouses fear; in contrast, master morality considers good precisely the one who inspires fear, and bad those who inspire contempt. It is clear that slave morality is characterized by love of freedom, whereas master morality, on the contrary, is characterized by respect for social hierarchy and veneration for rank.[197] The first attempt to clarify the dependence of different types of morality on class oppositions we already find in "Menschliches, Allzumenschliches".[198]

Slave morality is precisely the point of view that prevails in our time. The moral worldview of today represents the historical result of the struggle of two opposing ideals, two opposing evaluations of life. In the struggle of masters and slaves, Nietzsche sees the fundamental motive of all European history. By this struggle, he explains not only the genesis of morality but also the formation of religion, philosophical systems, and social and political ideals. Pagan antiquity for him is essentially the embodiment of the aristocratic ideal; on the contrary, Judaism and Christianity are the incarnation of everything slave-like. In these world religions, proclaiming "the equality of men before God," there was expressed, in his opinion, "the revolt of slaves against masters." The collapse of pagan Rome, the domination of the Church in the Middle Ages, the victory of the Reformation over the pagan spirit of the Renaissance, the fall of the empire of Napoleon I and the subsequent domination of democratic tendencies in European life – all these are stages of that historical process which in our days has led to the final triumph of the slaves – the mass of the weak – over the minority of the strong.

I need not enter into a detailed exposition of Nietzsche's purely historical views, but for a critical evaluation of his worldview it is essential to note the basic tendency of his philosophy of history: this tendency consists in reducing the historical process of Europe's development to a process of class struggle, with class opposition corresponding to the physiological – or more precisely anthropological – opposition of weak and strong races.

Here, we must note the point of contact between Nietzsche's doctrine and the worldview of Karl Marx, who, in other respects, appears to be the complete antithesis of our philosopher. Nietzsche's philosophy of history is a kind of "historical materialism." It coincides with Marxism in its denial of absolute moral principles, in its denial of ideas as prime movers of history, and in its explanation of morality through class oppositions. Nietzsche could have signed under the proposition of Marx and Engels that human ideals – moral, religious, social, and political – are "reflections of class struggle in human heads," "reflexes of social relations."

Most curious is that these philosophical-historical principles common to both thinkers lead them to diametrically opposite evaluations of concrete historical reality and to the justification of diametrically opposite practical aims. Nietzsche hates Christianity mainly as a bulwark of democracy, as the classical expression of the religious faith and morality of "slaves." Marx, on the contrary, hates Christianity for other reasons: he sees in it above all an instrument of exploitation of the lower by the higher, a bulwark of capitalism, "a reflection of commodity production"; from his side, he could instead call Christianity a "worldview of masters." Principles of historical materialism, similar in many respects, serve in Marx as a foundation of the socialist ideal; in Nietzsche, on the contrary, as an instrument of the overthrow of democracy. For Marx, historical materialism is above all a "philosophy of the proletariat"; for Nietzsche, it serves as support for the aristocratic ideal. Both thinkers see in history the manifestation of senseless, blind force. But on this basis, one of them believes in the future triumph of the mass power of the proletariat; the other hopes for the victory of the minority – the strongest varieties of humankind – the Overman.

CHAPTER: XV

The Positive Task of a Man

In destroying, Nietzsche also wants to create. All his critique of modern morality proceeds from a positive ideal, from the notion of the "true" values of life. What, then, are these actual values? Already from Nietzsche's negative judgments about modern humanity, religion, and morality, it is clear that he, above all, hates every manifestation of impotence: the only valid value for him is strength; only strength can confer value upon human existence.

Here Nietzsche's moral worldview is bound up with his metaphysics. We saw that for him, genuine being is strength, or, what is the same, the will to power. Hence follows the practical conclusion: in a world whose essence is striving for power, altruistic morality sounds like a sentimental falsehood; it appears as the summit of falsity and tastelessness.[199] One cannot sympathize with what is powerless and insignificant – Nietzsche's whole critique of the morality of compassion reduces to this. Man's task is to become himself a manifestation of strength: only under that condition can he be helpful to others as a majestic and beautiful spectacle. Instead of forever imposing ourselves on others with our clumsy and always superficial help, would it not be better if we made of ourselves something upon which others could look with delight: something like a garden, beautiful, tranquil, and enclosed within itself, fenced off by high walls from storms and street dust, and yet hospitable?[200]

What is valuable in man is his possible, future greatness, not his pitiful actuality. "In man there is creature and creator; in him there is matter, something unfinished (Bruchstück), excess, clay, filth, nonsense, chaos; but in man there is also creator, sculptor, hardness of hammer, divinity of contemplation, and the seventh day of rest. Do you understand this opposition? Do you feel that your compassion relates to the creature in man, to that which must be formed, broken, shackled, torn, burned, melted, and purified – to that which inevitably suffers and must suffer?"[201]

Strength knows no pity. To create a new, powerful type of man, one must not only refrain from helping one's neighbor but must even strive to hasten his downfall. "Everything present," says Zarathustra, "is falling, declining; perhaps someone would like to stop this fall, but I want to hasten it with a new push. Do you know the lust of him who throws stones into an abyss? Look at the men of today, how they roll into my abysses. My brothers, I am only a prologue: the drama will be played by actors better than I. After my example! Follow my example! And if you do not learn to fly, then learn at least quickly to fall!"[202]

Until now, the destruction of the weak has been delayed by the religion of compassion and mercy; in this, Nietzsche sees one of religion's greatest crimes against humanity: by preserving in life all the sick and weak, religion has thereby worsened our European race; it is the chief cause why the human type still remains on such a low level of development.[203] In such an understanding of compassion, there is expressed a misinterpreted love: if we truly love man, then we must wish the elevation of his type; we must love him not in his weak, but in his strong, beautiful specimens. "Remember this word," says Zarathustra, "every great love is above all your compassion, for it still wants to create that which it loves. 'To myself I bring my love, and to my neighbors – to those like me,' such are the words of all creators. But all creators are hard."[204] "Such is the demand of my love for the distant future: spare not your neighbor: man is something that must be overcome."[205]

Not softness of heart, but hardness must become the basic rule of conduct. "Why are you so soft, brothers?" says Zarathustra, "Why so evasive and yielding? Why so little negation and renunciation in your heart and so little doom in your gaze? And if you will not be inexorable as fate, how can you conquer with me? And if your hardness will not flash like lightning, dividing and cleaving, how can you create with me? For all creators are hard. And count it as bliss to imprint your hand upon millennia as upon wax, to stamp upon the will of millennia as upon bronze, harder than bronze. Only the noblest is completely hard. This new tablet I set before you, brothers: be hard."[206]

Such is the "morality of strength." In the world, there is no other Deity but strength.[207] Since all life is will to power, the value of every being, therefore of every man and human type, is measured by the degree of its power.[208] "I value man," says Nietzsche, "by the amount of his power and by the fullness of his will." The power of every will is measured by its strength of resistance, its ability to endure suffering and torture, to utilize suffering itself for its elevation.[209] Degrees of power differ, and therefore, values are unequal. Thus, the tablets of values, those new tablets Nietzsche wishes to substitute for the old, establish a definite hierarchical order: they represent nothing more nor less than a scale of forces. All other "values" are fruits of prejudice, misunderstanding, naïveté. The rise of one or another individual on the ladder of forces signifies for him an increase of value; conversely, the decrease of strength signifies a decrease of value.[210]

We saw earlier that in Nietzsche's eyes, sympathetic impulses serve as a sign of weakness, while self-love, elevated to a principle, on the contrary, is a sign of strength. But according to his own teaching, sympathy appears only as an expression of the refined egoism of weakness; and since egoism can embody both strength and weakness, it cannot be the measure of value: one egoism is not equal to another. "Egoism is valuable only insofar as the one who possesses it is physiologically valuable. Every man must be evaluated depending on whether he represents the ascending or descending line of life. If he represents the elevation of the line 'man,' then he possesses extraordinary value, since in him the general life of humanity makes a step forward; therefore, the concern for his preservation and growth must be exceptional: as a representative of the type of the future, he enjoys a special right to egoism. The individual is not something separated from the species: he cannot exist as a world enclosed in itself, standing outside general development; in each human individual is contained all the past, all the lines of man before him. Hence, the extraordinary value of successful specimens of the human race. On the contrary, if a man embodies in himself a descending line of development, decline, chronic illness, then his value is insignificant: elementary justice demands that he occupy as little space as possible, take away as little strength and sunlight as possible from successful specimens. In these cases, society is obliged to restrain the egoism of individuals and even of entire degenerating masses, for such egoism may turn out absurd, morbid, and rebellious."[211] A certain degree of illness entails the loss of the very right to life: the sick man is always a parasite of society, and therefore, there are sick people for whom it is indecent to live. Nietzsche advises holding physicians responsible for preserving diseased existences, which must be mercilessly eliminated in the interest of life itself – of ascending life.[212]

Evaluation of people by degree of power has nothing in common with the standard evaluation by degree of usefulness. To judge a person by whether he brings others benefit or harm is as absurd as judging a work of art by its practical results.[213] Such an evaluation leads to complete ignoring and distortion of all valid values of life. Thus, from the standpoint of usefulness, virtue receives a high rating; meanwhile, in reality, the "virtuous" are the lowest variety of the human race: they have no personality; all their merit lies in resembling a specific scheme "man," once and for all established; all their value is not in themselves, but in the species they serve; they are of little value because they are not unique in their kind and have many like themselves. If we value them, the fault lies in our laziness and our cowardice, which love quiet and safety.[214]

In Nietzsche's eyes, the good man is a décadent.[215] We have seen that, from his point of view, a man's strength is revealed not in good, but in evil, in the ability to resist the conventional, to "transgress" age-old customs. Every great man who brings something new into life inevitably "transgresses" the old law and therefore is a criminal, but a criminal in the grand, not the pitiful, style. The criminal is above all the type of the strong man, and therefore, he is the most valuable human type. If he does not repent, does not bewail his deed to please conventional morality, this is a sign of his mental health.[216]

The person whom people usually call a "criminal" is a type of strong man who has fallen into unfavorable conditions. In such conditions, any strong man will find himself within the pampered and degenerate milieu of modern society. He feels an attraction to freer and more dangerous forms of life, to everything that justifies the use of weapons and self-defense. All his virtues are under a ban in the eyes of society; all his life strivings are objects of horror and are branded with disgrace. If he is not strong enough to struggle with society, he must inevitably degenerate into the type of criminal in the ordinary sense of the word. There are, however, cases when a strong man gets the upper hand over society – such is the case of Napoleon; then he is called not a criminal but a great man. The seeds of the "criminal" lie in all those whom we single out, who rise above the general level – in great inventors, artists, scholars, in all geniuses in general. Every great innovator has at some time borne the brand of public condemnation and has lived the existence of a Catiline (Roman politician who instigated the Catilinarian conspiracy, a failed attempt to seize control of the Roman state in 63 BC), for he has felt hatred toward everything around him. "Catiline – this is the preliminary form of existence of every

Caesar!"²¹⁷ Nietzsche praises Dostoevsky for depicting, in his Notes from the House of the Dead, the convicts as the strongest and best Russian people.²¹⁸ At the same time, however, the fact goes unnoticed that Dostoevsky valued in the convicts not only a high level of gifts, but also those germs of good which he discovered in them: he valued in them especially that which, from Nietzsche's standpoint, deserves condemnation.

In connection with all the above, it becomes clear why Nietzsche bows before the greatest monster of the Renaissance – the famous Duke of Romagna, Cesare Borgia. It is known that this ruler marked his reign with a veritable orgy of cruelty: he terrorized his subjects with mass executions, killed not only those dangerous to him but also their children, so that there would be no one to avenge them; finally, he quartered his faithful servant who had carried out his orders, so that the people would attribute the executions to the latter and not to the duke himself. And this very Cesare Borgia Nietzsche calls "a great virtuoso of life." This man, he says, is of course one of those whom the Church sends to hell; but there sit the greatest of the German emperors, and in general all great men. It is known that there are no interesting people in heaven at all.²¹⁹

The Renaissance abounded in such "interesting people," and therefore, in Nietzsche's eyes, it is the classical epoch of the flowering of the human personality. Compared with the age of Cesare Borgia, our age, with its morality of altruism, represents a step back. We think that, in a moral respect, our epoch is infinitely higher than the Renaissance. Of course, we cannot even in thought transport ourselves into the conditions of that epoch; our nerves would not withstand such a reality, to say nothing of our muscles. But this incapacity proves no progress at all, only a different constitution, later and therefore weaker, more pampered, more sensitive; this is the soil on which a morality rich in concern for others is born. If we abstract from our belatedness, softness, and old age, then our morality of "humanization" at once loses all value (in itself, no morality has any value); we will even treat it with disdain. There is no doubt that we moderns, with our humanity padded with a thick layer of cotton so as not to bump into any stones, would provide to the contemporaries of Cesare Borgia a spectacle at which they would die laughing.[220]

Nietzsche's morality – if one can call his teaching on conduct a morality at all – recognizes as the highest value everything that Christianity denies. He himself thus defines the content of his "opposite ideal": he elevates to a principle pride, the sense of distance between higher and lower, great responsibility, arrogance, the magnificence of animal life (die prachtvolle Animalität), warlike and conquering instincts, the deification of passion, revenge, cunning, anger, lust, the thirst for adventure and knowledge. This is the aristocratic ideal of a beautiful, wise, powerful, and dangerous human type – the type of the future.[221]

Aristocratism lies at the basis of Nietzsche's moral doctrine as well as at the basis of his social and political views, with which we are to become acquainted; but before following him into this field, let us attempt a critical analysis of the doctrine of morality just set forth.

CHAPTER: XVI

Needless to say, this doctrine, like Nietzsche's philosophy as a whole, swarms with contradictions. Above all, it wants to stand outside morality, outside the opposition of good and evil, "to be immoral, like nature itself".[222] But we must once again be convinced that this immoralism in Nietzsche is not consistent. External nature, which, in his view, ought to serve as our model, really does stand outside the opposition of good and evil; but this obviously means that nature is indifferent to good and evil: if it is incapable of compassion, it also knows neither anger nor condemnation; foreign to it are any notions of duty and non-duty, of value and non-value. Therefore, if we want to be like nature, we must renounce all preferences, all evaluations, and values whatsoever. Consistent immoralism is at the same time complete indifferentism. Such was Spinoza's point of view, who taught that one must "neither laugh, nor weep, but understand."

It is clear to everyone that Nietzsche's philosophy, with its "new tablets of values," has nothing in common with such indifferentism. In it, there is joy and sorrow, laughter and tears, admiration and indignation. With reference to the above words of Spinoza, Nietzsche himself notes that each of our judgments expresses an evaluation of reality: all our understanding of existence is the result of a certain compromise between ridicule, lamentation, and curse.[223]

Since Nietzsche's philosophy recognizes strength as good and weakness as evil, it is evident that it does not stand outside the opposition of good and evil, but only tries to put into these concepts a new content, different from the conventional. Nietzsche often repeats that his indignation against modern humanity is not moral condemnation, that it is free of morality. In fact, it is free of the prevailing morality, i.e., of altruistic, Christian morality; but this does not mean that it is free of all moral evaluation whatsoever, for any indignation or condemnation is possible only from the standpoint of some definite idea of good and evil. Nietzsche himself admits that his slogan "beyond good and evil," which served as the title for one of his works, does not mean "beyond good and bad".[224]

Apparently, Nietzsche locates the difference of his teaching from everything called "morality" in the fact that it contains no unconditional principles of conduct, whereas all morality rests on the idea of the absolutely obligatory, the absolutely due. And indeed, we have seen that he does not recognize any "one saving" morality, any principles of conduct that would have universal significance. The infinite diversity of human characters and talents must correspond to a diversity of prescriptions, a multiplicity of moralities.

If one adopts this point of view, then all criticism in the field of morality becomes impossible. If there is nothing unconditionally obligatory, then the choice of one or another behavior becomes a matter of personal discretion and taste: then, suitable for each is what he regards as good. But if so, what right do we have to assert that one principle of conduct is better and another worse? What right does Nietzsche have to assert that self-love is better than compassion and disinterested love for one's neighbor? If there are no unconditional criteria above our lives, we have no grounds to prefer one human type to another. From this standpoint, there can be no scale of values whatsoever; if so, then of course the Christian evaluation of the merciful Samaritan and the hardhearted Levite appears untenable; but to the same degree, untenable is Nietzsche's thesis that the strong is better than the weak.

At the basis of Nietzsche's moral doctrine lies such a contradiction: on the one hand, he denies the existence of values that could have significance as unconditional, universal norms of conduct; on the other hand, he teaches that the only valid value is strength, power: all other values recognized by men are "fruits of prejudice and naïveté." The very attempt at a "revaluation of all values," in other words, Nietzsche's whole moral philosophy, presupposes precisely what he denies – the existence of the one true, and therefore unconditional and universal, value, in opposition to those spurious values recognized hitherto.

On the one hand, we are told that the very concept of value is partly a fiction, an invention of man, and partly a "delusion of the organic world"; that our very life is something contrary to nature, since it introduces into nature a notion of value alien to it;[225] on the other hand, we encounter the assertion that valid values are rooted in the structure of the universe: they are given by nature itself.

This contradiction is linked with Nietzsche's typical vacillation in his critical judgments; on the one hand, he rejects and condemns all morality as such; on the other hand, he sympathizes with what he calls "sound morality," i.e., naturalism in morality. Sound, from his point of view, is that moral doctrine which is guided by the instinct of life, that morality which elevates to a canon of duty everything that furthers the increase of life and brands as not-to-be-done everything that is destructive to it. By contrast, unnatural morality is that which turns against the instinct of life, denies life: to this belong almost all those moral teachings that have hitherto been preached.

At the basis of this opposition of two moralities lies Nietzsche's contradictory relation to nature. On the one hand, for him, nature is everything, and therefore, there can be nothing opposed to nature. From this point of view, it would seem one cannot speak of opposition between the natural and the unnatural in man: our entire psyche, all our instincts and judgments are manifestations of nature, and therefore everything in us is equally natural. On the other hand, however, man appears as something alien to nature, as a kind of dissonance within it. Everything in him is unnatural, and Nietzsche demands man's return to nature.

For this, man must renounce imaginary, spurious values and accept those values given by nature itself.

But here arises a further question: can nature serve as the criterion for distinguishing true from spurious values? Everything Nietzsche says on this subject is fundamentally contradictory: on the one hand, in him, nature acquires the significance of the supreme measure of values, by which correct evaluation must be guided; on the other hand, it turns out that nature establishes all our tablets of values whatsoever, both true and false. The morality of altruism is dictated by the instincts of our life just as much as the opposite morality of egoism. When we value everything that serves the preservation of our personality and the increase of our power, there speaks in us the instinct of ascending life; conversely, when we preach the morality of self-renunciation and self-denial, we follow the instinct of declining life.[226]

From the point of view of consistent naturalism, all our instincts must be recognized as equally natural and therefore equally valuable: "nature" itself cannot give us any logical grounds for preferring some instincts to others. Meanwhile, in Nietzsche, instincts are far from equally evaluated. He admits that "all that is good in us is instinct," but he is far from considering every instinct good: man, especially modern man, is for him a being with perverted instincts. If contemporary humanity, he says, were left to its instincts, this could have fatal consequences for it. "These instincts contradict one another, paralyze and destroy one another; I define modernity as physiological self-contradiction."[227]

Hence it is evident that in Nietzsche the very criterion of value splits in two: on the one hand, he tends to identify the valuable with the natural; on the other hand, it turns out that not all that is natural is valuable; instincts require the supreme control of consciousness; valuable in them is only what endures the critique of reason, only what reason acknowledges as strong and powerful.

Nietzsche's identification of value with power is itself inconsistent: the cult of strength or of the "will to power" cannot be reconciled with the individualism of his philosophy. In fact, the species is always more potent than the individual; the herd, as a whole, is always more substantial than a single member. If we abstract from all other considerations and value only strength as such, then we must always give preference to the species, to the manifestations of its collective power. Nietzsche's cult of the independent personality, detached from society, stands in radical contradiction with his cult of strength: if the scale of values is the same as the scale of forces, then we must value not those human qualities that exalt the individual at the expense of society, but rather those that turn the individual into an instrument of the whole, that strengthen society, even at the expense of the individual; from this point of view, "herd morality" deserves every preference over the morality of egoism; what Nietzsche calls the "degeneration" and "decline" of the individual is more valuable than what he sees as its flourishing. The duality of Nietzsche's scale of values is most clearly revealed in his condemnation of every manifestation of the power of society, the state; he sees in them evil. Concerning the triumph of the Germans over the French and the unification of Germany, he directly says that "power stupefies":[228] the success of the Germans, as a nation, is harmful because it makes the individual foolish.

This is connected with the contradiction already noted in his evaluation of human reason. The duality of Nietzsche's ethical teaching lies precisely in his continual wavering between preference for reason and for strength. When he takes the biological point of view, reason appears to him as an instrument of organic life, something very superficial and insignificant compared with this life as a whole. But on the other hand, in Nietzsche, there remain vestiges of an idealistic faith in reason.

We saw that for him, knowledge is the dearest thing in life – that which makes life valuable: it is higher than happiness, more precious than peace. The highest goal to which reason strives is the knowledge of truth. And here, in evaluating this goal, we find in Nietzsche the same typical vacillation. Taking the biological point of view, he concludes that "the preference of truth over error is the purest prejudice," for error contributes more than knowledge to the growth of man's power. More than that, reason, with its quest for truth, is dangerous to life, because it destroys the presuppositions necessary for it, those illusions on which it rests.[229] It kills animal energy: people who live a conscious life are, compared with others, sickly creatures, vessels more fragile and delicate;[230] error is as necessary to us as the skin that protects us from harmful external influences.[231]

And yet in Nietzsche there is something higher than this "biological" point of view, something that makes him exalt the search for truth into the supreme principle of conduct. From a biological perspective, would not that unreasoning faith which gives us strength to endure suffering and serves as a source of vital energy be better? And yet Nietzsche glorifies love of truth, "intellectual conscientiousness," as the highest quality of man, as a sacred "duty" from which even the immoralist is not permitted to deviate! His chief reproach against modern religion is the reproach of dishonesty. However, "saving for life" this or that teaching may be, Nietzsche holds in contempt anyone who accepts it without intellectual scrutiny.[232] As is clear from the preceding citations, both opposite evaluations of reason occur in the same work of Nietzsche and therefore cannot be attributed to different periods of his activity. To renounce thought means to renounce that which justifies human existence.

From the biological point of view, Nietzsche values everything that promotes "the increase of the splendor of animal life," everything that cultivates in man the "fine specimen of the animal." He cannot forgive Christianity above all for the fact that, with its asceticism, it killed in man the energy of animal life. But such are the contradictions of his thought that alongside this, he especially cherishes precisely that which separates man from the animals, namely, the independence of the personality free from the herd instinct. "Upon man," he says, "many chains have been laid so that he might unlearn to behave like a beast, and in truth, he has become gentler, more spiritual, more joyful, more reasonable than any animal. But now he also suffers from having worn his chains too long, from having so long lacked pure air and freedom of movement. These chains, I repeat, are the heavy and many-meaning errors of moral, religious, and metaphysical conceptions. Only after overcoming this sickness of chains will the first great goal be attained – the separation of man from the animals."[233]

Such are the opposing tendencies that contend in Nietzsche's moral philosophy: he wants at once to cultivate the beast in man and to dig a chasm between man and animal. That we have here a contradiction, and not two different tendencies corresponding to different periods of Nietzsche's work, is evident from the following. It is known that the glorification of the "splendor of animal life" belongs to the epoch of "Zarathustrism"; it found its most striking expression in Nietzsche's posthumous work Der Wille zur Macht.[234] Yet in the same epoch Nietzsche continued to dream of separating man from the animal: he saw in man a transitional form, "a rope stretched between animal and overman."[235] The exact oppositions and the same contradictions lie at the basis of his social and political views.

CHAPTER: XVII

Social and Political Views of Nietzsche

We have already seen that moral conceptions, from Nietzsche's standpoint, are reflections of social relations. Altruistic morality is the expression of a democratic mode of life and of democratic tendencies within society. By contrast, that morality which Nietzsche calls "sound," "naturalistic," "master-morality," is the creation of the higher strata of society – of conquering masters – of the aristocracy.

Therefore, the evaluation of one or another morality for Nietzsche is at the same time an evaluation of one or another social type, of the social order which created each given morality. Behind his hatred of altruistic morality lies a profound contempt for everything stamped with democracy. All his social and political views are built from beginning to end upon aristocratic principles.

We have already seen that to his hierarchy of values corresponds a hierarchy of forces in human society. Men are not equal by nature, and therefore not equal in value; hence, it would be the height of madness and injustice to equalize them in rights. True justice consists in unequal treatment of unequal magnitudes, therefore in inequality,[236] in the predominance of the higher type.

Flowing from the elementary requirements of justice, the aristocratic order is at the same time the necessary condition of the highest cultural development. "Every elevation of the human type has hitherto been the work of an aristocratic society. So it will be in the future, for this goal requires such a society as believes in many hierarchical degrees, believes in the different worth of different men, and needs slaves in one sense or another of the word."[237] That man may continually grow upward, the habit of command must enter his very flesh and blood: he must be surrounded by slaves – tools of his will; he must be separated from the lower by the feeling of distance. The higher must not abase itself to the level of an instrument for the lower: the pathos of distance must forever divide the very tasks of men. Higher men have a thousand times more right to existence than the lower: this is the superiority of the bell with a full tone over the bell cracked and out of tune. In the higher men is the pledge of the future; they alone are bound by obligations toward the future of humanity.[238]

What, then, are the marks of the higher type, of those who have the right to command, as opposed to those who must obey? We have already seen that, according to Nietzsche, at the root of the contrast of masters and slaves lies the opposition of predatory and domestic animals, lambs and eagles. Every higher culture began always with conquest: some tribe of predators – barbarians in the complete sense of the word – would hurl themselves upon a peaceful shepherd or agricultural population, or upon a society with a decaying culture; after the conquest, the barbarians became the masters, the conquered population – the slaves. Such is the historical basis of every aristocracy. The masters at first surpassed the slaves not by physical strength, but by their psychic qualities: they were more whole men, or, which is the same, "more whole beasts".[239]

In this lies the justification of their rule. It is no wonder that lambs hate eagles and call them evil, but, on the other hand, one must not blame the eagles for making food of the tender and tasty lambs.[240] So it always was, and so it always will be. There exist many different forms, many different types of mastery and servitude. The very modes of exploitation of man by man change historically, but the essence remains unaltered. In our day, the opinion is widespread that in the future, a social condition will come in which exploitation will no longer occur. According to Nietzsche, to arrange society thus is as unthinkable as to create life without any organic functions. "Exploitation is not a characteristic of a corrupted or imperfect and primitive society; it is a basic feature of life, serves as its fundamental organic function"; it expresses that "will to power which constitutes the essence of all that exists."[241]

Therefore, the higher, better men must not be ashamed of exploitation. The essence of a good and healthy aristocracy lies in seeing itself not as a function of society, but as its justification and meaning: therefore, it must with an untroubled conscience accept the sacrifice of countless men who for its sake become incomplete men, slaves, instruments. It must be filled with the conviction that society must exist not for its own sake, but solely as a foundation and scaffolding upon which the higher race of beings may rise to its highest task. Such are the light-hungry climbing plants on the island of Java, known as Sipo Matador; they twine their branches about the oak until finally, raised above it yet leaning upon it, they unfold their crown in the free light, displaying their happiness.[242]

CHAPTER: XVIII

Such is not the prevailing tendency of our time. The characteristic feature of our epoch is the extraordinarily rapid democratization of society. All class distinctions are being erased and destroyed; men become entirely alike; in the struggle for existence, the ordinary man, the one who differs in nothing from the rest, gains the upper hand; by contrast, men of refined gifts, exceptional, rare specimens, remain misunderstood, isolated, and perish in their solitude. Enormous forces would be needed to arrest this natural process of assimilation (progressus in simile), the transformation of humanity into something ordinary, mediocre, herd-like, and vulgar![243] In general, nothing helps here: mankind cannot move backwards like a crab; it must step by step advance along the path of decline – this is the essence of modern "progress." Any attempts to hinder this movement can only result in its gathering and concentrating its forces, like a dammed river, in order to break through later with still greater energy.[244]

Surveying all possible strata of modern society, Nietzsche sees everywhere the same cheerless picture of general decline. The working class is completely depersonalized: workers do not regard it as shameful to play the part of cogs in a machine and, as it were, to fill up with themselves the gaps in human inventiveness. They feel no aversion to the thought that the essence of their suffering, their impersonal slavery, might be abolished by an increase of wages. More than that, they obey those theorists who teach that the disgrace of slavery can be turned into virtue by increasing this impersonality in the machine production of modern society. Their baseness goes so far that they agree, for a definite compensation, to cease being persons and to turn into cogs. Meanwhile, no payment is able to compensate the worker for the loss of his inner worth.

Hopes for a socialist order in the future are mad and senseless, for on the day when the worker ceases to be a slave of the capitalists, he will still be a slave of the revolutionary party, a slave of the new state, of the machine.[245] The significance of labor reduces to this – that it kills personality in the worker. From this point of view, the modern glorification of labor becomes understandable: at its basis lies fear of personality. In essence, now everyone feels that heavy, exhausting work, continuing from morning to night, is more effective than any police, since it serves as a bridle for everyone: it restrains the development of mind, of needs, of the sense of independence, since it consumes an enormous portion of the nervous system, diverting it from reflection, thought, dreams, cares, love, and hatred. It sets no goal before man, gives him cheap and constant satisfaction. Therefore, in a society where continuous, intensified labor is carried on, life is safe, and safety is the deity worshiped by modern man. And suddenly – horror! Precisely, the worker has become dangerous! Dangerous personalities swarm everywhere. And behind them lurks the greatest of all dangers, individuality.[246]

The labor question, which now stands before mankind in all its formidable grandeur, is the result of the prevailing tendency of our epoch – the striving for universal leveling and classlessness. To preserve the existing social order, one would have to cultivate in the worker a Chinese temperament – the type of the industrious and unpretentious ant. Instead, what has modern society done? It has erased class boundaries and, at the root, destroyed all those instincts by virtue of which the worker is possible as a class, possible for himself in this quality. Workers were called up for military service, given the right of association, and political voting rights. What wonder, then, if at present the worker sees in his condition a misfortune, or, expressed in moral language, an injustice. "But again, we must ask, what do we finally want? If we desire the end, we must desire the means; if we want to have slaves, we are fools if we educate them masters."[247]

The masters themselves are at present scarcely much better than the slaves. If we look into the milieu of the well-to-do and educated, here too we see a picture of decline, the debasement of intellectual interests, and general diminishment of personality. Modern society is infected with Americanism; there is something savage in that greed for gold which characterizes modern Americans and more and more infects modern Europe. More and more frequently, the type of man wholly absorbed in money affairs appears: in pursuit of profit, he knows no rest; he is ashamed of leisure, feels pangs of conscience when thought distracts him from the day's current concerns. We are gradually accustoming ourselves to think with a watch in hand; we breakfast with the stock-exchange sheet before our eyes; we live as if afraid to lose a minute for some important business. Fear of idleness, unceasing anxiety for the accumulation of wealth, and care for daily bread threaten to kill all culture and higher taste. We gradually lose the sense of form, the feeling for melody, and for all that is beautiful. In relations between men, a businesslike manner and rational clarity prevail; we have unlearned to rejoice in life; we count it a virtue "to do as much as possible in as little time as possible." When we spend time on a walk, in conversation with friends, or in the enjoyment of art, we already feel the need to justify it by "necessity of rest" or "requirements of hygiene." Soon, the very inclination to a contemplative life will fall into contempt. How much more exalted was the mood of the ancients! The ancient Greeks held the goal of life in contemplation; only war and contemplative life were considered worthy of the free; by contrast, labor was regarded as a servile occupation, worthy of contempt.[248]

Our age sets itself the goal of making man as useful as possible; for this, he must first of all be endowed with the virtues of an infallible machine: he must value above all the minutes of "mechanically useful labor." The chief stumbling block here is, of course, the boredom connected with such activity. To turn man into a "useful machine," he must be accustomed to boredom, even endowed with a special relish for it; herein lies the task of the modern school. This school compels us to learn precisely what does not concern us at all, to see in this allegedly "objective" activity our duty, to value duty independently of pleasure – this is its "inestimable merit"! Therefore, the philologist has been hitherto the educator par excellence, for his activity offers a classical example of monotony on a grand scale. From him, youth learns that mechanical performance of duties, which is the necessary quality of the future official, husband, slave of some office, newspaper reader, and soldier.[249]

CHAPTER: XIX

Our intellectual powers are exhausted: it is no wonder that the absence of any original style characterizes our age. In our impotence to create anything new, anything native in art, philosophy, or morality, we turn to the past, carefully collecting the fragments of outlived cultures. Hence, the predominance of historicism, of historical interest, which distinguishes modernity. Earlier epochs – antiquity, the Middle Ages, the Renaissance – possessed a distinctive style in architecture, sculpture, and in their whole intellectual life. By contrast, modernity is above all an epoch of imitation and comparison of all possible styles, customs, worldviews, and cultures.[250] It is a motley carnival – a mixture of the costumes of all possible times, of creeds, moralities, and religions.[251] The modern man is like those planets which borrow their light not from one but from several suns; in our activity, no single morality predominates, but several; hence our actions are tinted in varied colors, and we often commit motley deeds.[252]

There is no spiritual food which the modern man does not digest: in this lies his pride; but he would belong to a higher order of beings if he were deprived of this ability: the omnivorous man is by no means the most refined variety of man.[253] All this mixing of heterogeneous cultures, all our "historical sense," of which we boast so much, is a consequence of that semi-barbarous condition into which Europe has sunk owing to democratic mingling of estates and races. For the first time in the nineteenth century, historical sense has become something like a "sixth sense" of the educated man: this sense means a flair and taste for everything in the world, or, what is the same, the absence of refined and noble taste, a plebeian curiosity. What is the god of modern art, Shakespeare, if not the combination of all possible tastes? – a combination of Spanish with Moorish and Saxon, at which the ancient Athenians – the contemporaries of Aeschylus – would have died of laughter. And we, on the contrary, enjoy this wild motley, this mixture of delicate, coarse, and artificial, as the highest kind of art; we do not disdain to breathe the same air as the English mob – that atmosphere in which Shakespeare's creativity lives. Lack of taste is the reverse side of our receptivity and responsiveness.[254]

Being a mixed being, the modern man is at the same time something unfinished, a fragment, and a beginning of something. Our time, more than any other, is characterized by the development of specialization: as a result of the colossal growth of various branches of knowledge, education becomes less and less general; it acquires a fragmentary character; rich and deep natures no longer find suitable educators. The fractional man, the one-sided observer with arrogant pretensions – this is the modern cultural type. Today's universities have become a true school of lowering the intellectual level.[255]

Not only scientific specialists, but the majority of men represent, as it were, fragments, parts of man; to obtain the whole man, one must combine them. Entire epochs, entire nations, are examples of such one-sided development; all these lower human types are, as it were, anticipations and preludes to the higher: in their totality they prepare the appearance of those synthetic personalities which, like milestones, show how far humanity has advanced in its movement.[256]

In *Zarathustra*, we find the same thought expressed in the following figurative form. Once, being surrounded by cripples and maimed men, Zarathustra addressed them with these words: "One has no eye, another no ear, a third no leg; some have lost tongue, nose, or head. But this is far from the worst of what I have seen in men.

I see and have seen something worse, and sometimes so dreadful that I cannot speak of it all, and about some I must keep silent; I have seen men who lacked absolutely everything, but at the same time had too much of some one thing – for example, such men as are nothing but an enormous eye, or an enormous snout, or an enormous belly – something enormous in general. Such I call 'cripples inside out.'

Truly, my brothers, I wander among men as among the parts and organs of man. Most fearful to my sight is this – that I see man torn into pieces and scattered, as on a battlefield or in a slaughterhouse."[257]

These words apply to the most diverse human types – to modern artists and craftsmen who have one-sidedly developed some single ability, to specialists in all fields, but above all – to scholars. In every "specialist," says Nietzsche, what strikes one is a certain narrowness of view, the exaggerated optics of the little corner where he sits, and – his hump – every specialist has one. In every scholarly book, a crooked soul is reflected, for every craft warps! Every mastery in the world is acquired at a heavy price: whoever wishes to master his craft must in the end become its victim. Such is precisely the fate of scholarly specialists: they grow into their corner, lose balance, become thin, angular in everything except their one specialty.[258] Their exclusively study-bound life entails a loss of receptivity and intellectual freshness. "If you touch them with your hands," says Zarathustra, "they give off dust, like sacks of flour; and one might think this dust came from grain, from the grace and gold of fields." "They are good clockworks; only they must be wound up in time; then they show the time without deception, and at the same time modestly tick. They work like mills and mortars, only grain must be thrown to them! They know well how to grind grain into the finest parts and turn it into white dust."[259]

All these qualities of the scholar betray in him a type ignoble, democratic: he has none of the virtues of those who rule, who command, who are self-sufficient. His virtues – diligence, patience, persistence, obedience to discipline, the habit of reckoning with others as equals – betray in him a dependent, herd being.²⁶⁰ That is why Zarathustra cannot endure scholars. "Too long," he says, "has my soul hungered at their table; for me knowledge is not, as for them, the cracking of nuts."²⁶¹

In the modern development of specialized knowledge at the expense of general philosophical interests, Nietzsche sees the manifestation of the vulgar tendencies of the age. "The declaration of independence by the man of learning, his emancipation from philosophy, represents one of the subtlest expressions of the democratic spirit and discord." "'Away with all masters!' – so plebeian instinct wills here as well. After science ceased to be 'the handmaid of theology,' the arrogance and unreason of the man of learning now wishes in turn to dictate laws to philosophy, to lord it over her. More than that, scholars themselves wish to be philosophers. Most often among scholars, one may notice a contemptuous attitude toward all philosophy whatever, joined to slavish dependence upon some single philosophical doctrine which serves the scholar as an object of unreasoning, naïve faith."

To this disenchantment with philosophy, modern philosophers themselves have largely contributed, with their lack of creativity and understanding of the great synthetic tasks of thought. Especially those "mixed men" who call themselves positivists or "philosophers of reality" are able to instill dangerous distrust into the soul of the young scholar. At best, these philosophers are themselves "specialists," men of learning: not being capable of it, they have taken up the regal tasks of philosophy. And now they avenge their impotence, preaching in word and deed distrust of philosophy.²⁶²

Democratization and the vulgarization of thought connected with it are evident not only in the decline of modern philosophical systems, but also in the distortion of scientific thought itself, for in its fundamental definitions, the positive sciences are unavoidably dependent on philosophy. Nietzsche points out traces of democratism in sociology,²⁶³ biology,²⁶⁴ and even in physics.[265]

In a word, in all spheres of intellectual and moral life, one and the same process – the decline of culture – is taking place with incredible rapidity. What causes it? In particular, what contributes to the decline of German culture? Above all, higher education has lost the character of a privilege – this is the democratization of accessible, universal education. Nor should one forget that privileges of military service directly compel the overcrowding of higher schools, that is, their ruin. Now in modern Germany, no one can give their children an aristocratic education: all higher schools, with their teachers, curricula, and aims, are adapted to the most dubious mediocrity.[266]

CHAPTER: XX

Ordinarily, in refutation of all talk about the decline of culture, people point to the colossal progress of the state principle. For Nietzsche, on the contrary, the very growth of the state is both a symptom and a cause of decline, for the state embodies the collective, the herd principle. Culture and state are antagonists: the state can prosper only at the expense of culture, and culture only at the expense of the state. Everything great in the cultural sense is alien to politics; conversely, the state, once it has attained power, ceases to be the center of cultural life. Intellectual life flourished in Germany at the beginning of the nineteenth century, when the country was politically insignificant; after the political unification of Germany, the center of cultural movement shifted to defeated France.[267] From this standpoint Zarathustra teaches that the state is the "death of peoples," an institution for the "superfluous"; the type of the true, "non-superfluous" man begins where the state ends.[268]

As is social life, so are political theories. They provide formulas for the distorted instincts of degenerate European society. What are the fundamental aims of socialism? It is in all respects the fantastic younger brother of dying despotism. It demands for itself such completeness of state power as far surpasses anything of despotism's past; it strives directly toward the annihilation of individuality, which it sees as an inopportune luxury in nature; and so socialism seeks to turn the individual into a purposive organ of collective life. The power of the Caesars would have been far from sufficient for this goal, for socialism demands a hitherto unheard-of submissive devotion of all citizens to the unlimited power of the state.[269]

At bottom, liberal doctrines rest on the same foundation. Liberal institutions "undermine" the striving of the individual for power, level hills and valleys, make men small, cowardly, greedy for pleasures: in them the herd animal triumphs. Liberalism is nothing other than herd-formation. Nations that have counted for something have never achieved greatness under liberal institutions: great danger has forged from them something worthy of respect – that danger in which our strength, our martial virtue, our spirit is awakened. Liberal institutions, once secured, ruin the higher qualities of human nature precisely because they create an atmosphere of universal security.[270] All modern political institutions, constitutions, and theories, from liberalism to anarchism, express different sides of one and the same decline; they all converge in their common attachment to the ideal of the "autonomous herd" and in their common hostility to every other social order resting on the opposition of slaves and masters.[271]

The general dream of demagogues is the happiness of a green pasture for all, with calm, safety, comfort, and ease of life for each; their favorite doctrine is "equality of rights" and "compassion for all sufferers." For them, suffering is something to be abolished. But we, Nietzsche says, think the plant "man" grows tallest under opposite conditions: for that, the danger of his situation must be raised to the extreme. Cruelty, violence, slavery, danger in the street and heart, stoicism, the art of temptation and devilry of every kind, the predatory and the serpentine in man – these are the qualities that above all elevate the human race.[272]

At the root of modern political ideals, as of the morality of compassion, lies the same source – slave revolt against masters. In Nietzsche's eyes, the demagogy of the modern age is best embodied in Rousseau, who was at once an idealist and a scoundrel, a preacher of equality out of malice and envy toward everything that rises above the common level.[273]

In the end, all this democratism is nothing but the historical continuation of the idealization of the weak, the "feeble of this world," which began already in Christianity. Christianity first proclaimed the equality of all before God! "The first and the last

Christian," Nietzsche says, "rises up to gratify the lower instinct against all privilege: he lives and fights for equal rights."[274] The Christian and the anarchist – in equal measure – are decadents. The Christian condemns and reviles the world under the pressure of the same instinct that makes the socialist worker revile, slander, and condemn modern society. The "most dreadful garden" itself is the delight of anticipated revenge; it is the same revolution the socialist worker dreams of, only projected farther into the future.[275]

Diminution and degeneration in modern Europe have gone so far that the very type of the independent man, the ruler, is gradually disappearing. Europe is under the spell of the widespread prejudice that the herdlike, obedient man is the only permitted type. Hence, rulers themselves, compelled to command others, feel pangs of conscience in doing so: to be able to command, they must resort to self-deception. This is what Nietzsche calls "the hypocrisy of rulers." In giving orders, rulers pretend as if they commanded not in their own name, but as if they too obeyed older imperatives, for example, the traditions of ancestors, prescriptions of constitution, law, right, or even of God: they wish to persuade all that they themselves follow the rules of herd-wisdom as "first servants of the people" or "instruments of the common good." The very constitutional form of rule in modern states is permeated with the same spirit: contemporary parliamentarism is nothing but an attempt to replace true, innate rulers with the collective wisdom of many herd-men.[276]

CHAPTER: XXI

Nietzsche's social philosophy, like his moral teaching, is permeated with aversion to man. What explains this aversion, he asks himself, "for without any doubt, we suffer on account of man? The cause here is not fear, but rather that we have nothing left to fear from man: man – the worm – has occupied the entire foreground and swarms everywhere; the tame and hopelessly mediocre man has already learned to see in himself the higher man, the final goal, the summit and meaning of history."[277]

In this somber light, Nietzsche sees not only the present but also the past of mankind. "When my gaze turns from the present to the past," says Zarathustra, "it finds there the very same thing: scattered parts, organs of man, but men it does not see. The present and the past on earth, my brothers, that is for me the most unbearable; I would not know how to live, if I were not a seer of the future."[278]

Nietzsche's consolation lies in the fact that he sees in the present a transition to a better future. "A seer, a willing one, a man of the future, and as it were a bridge to the future – but at the same time, alas, as it were a cripple upon this bridge – such is Zarathustra."[279] The guarantee of that better future which Zarathustra foresees lies in the very process of degeneration of modern humanity. This terrifying decline represents the necessary prelude to that great growth which humanity has before it. When the old crumbles and perishes, it means that a new, higher form of existence is being born. Suffering itself, the symptoms of decline, foretell epochs of intensified forward movement. When the higher man grows, so too must grow his reverse side, the ordinary, lower man: the elevation of rare, exceptional specimens requires contrast.[280] From this point of view, the degeneration of humanity must be seen in a new light. Fall, decline, and degeneration are not things deserving of condemnation;

they are the necessary consequences of life itself and of its growth. The phenomenon of "decadence" is as necessary as every ascent of life, every forward step: it is not within our power to stop it. On the contrary, reason seeks its justification.[281]

The justification lies in the fact that for the higher race of beings, the lower are necessary, as instruments and a pedestal: more precisely, for masters, slaves are necessary. The diminishment of man over a long span of time must be considered the sole aim of history: only in this way can a broad and solid foundation be created upon which a stronger variety of man will shine.[282]

From this perspective, one ought not to delay, but rather to accelerate the process of universal leveling now taking place in Europe. As soon as this process reaches its end, the diminished human herd will of itself fall into the hands of the strong – their natural lords and rulers. For the more the mass diminishes, the wider grows the chasm between it and the higher variety of man; the greater, therefore, becomes the preponderance of power on the side of the latter.

The justification of the crowd lies in its service to the higher race of rulers, who, without it, could not fulfill their task. The task of the ruling race consists not merely in governing: its goal is not in the governed, not in the lower, but in itself, in its own sphere of life. Here, it must be a phenomenon of abundance – of strength, beauty, courage, highest culture, and style. It is a self-affirming and life-joyful breed of men, who can afford every luxury, strong enough not to need the tyranny of moral commandments, rich enough not to be thrifty or pedantic – beyond good and evil. It is, as it were, a conservatory filled with rare and exquisite plants.[283]

Thus, modern human development leads to a twofold result: it prepares the type of man-machine, it seeks to transform humanity into an immense system of wheels and levers fitted to each other and adapted to the common goal of production. In preparing in this way splendid instruments of exploitation, modern civilization thereby prepares the conditions of existence for a new type of exploiters. Modern machine production drives the exploitation of man by man to its maximum: this exploitation will not disappear, but will find its justification in the future, when a new nobility is born, worthy to rule over the lower.[284]

Between "masters" and "slaves" there will also be room for men of middling gifts: higher culture can rest only upon the broad foundation of a firmly united mediocrity. For it, scholars are above all necessary; but science has never been an aristocratic occupation: it cannot coexist with the exceptional gifts of genius, but at the same time it is not the business of the mass; it is exactly suited to the middle type of men. To conduct trade and handle capital, once more, men with bourgeois inclinations are needed, in other words, men of middling gifts.[285]

Since higher culture cannot dispense with slaves, that morality which cultivates in man the qualities of an instrument appears necessary and desirable. I declared war on the Christian ideal, Nietzsche says, not at all in order to destroy it, but in order to put an end to its tyranny and clear space for other, more powerful ideals. The continued existence of the Christian worldview in itself is even highly desirable. "We, the immoralists, need the power of morality: our striving for self-preservation requires that our opponents remain strong; it only seeks to rule over them."[286] From Nietzsche's point of view, the rule is the necessary condition of the existence of exceptions.[287] In order that higher men be perfect masters, it is necessary that the mass be a perfect herd.

CHAPTER: XXII

After all that has already been said about the inner contradictions of Nietzsche's moral philosophy, criticism of his social and political teaching can be reduced to a few remarks. Here we find the same contradictions, the same dual scale of values.

Most dual in character is the very concept of "decline," under which Nietzsche subsumes all contemporary social development. "Decline" in his usage means now a falling away from a particular norm of biological perfection once attained in the past, in the age of the flourishing "blond beast," now a deviation from the ideal of higher rationality attainable only in the future. As a result, the same facts are understood by Nietzsche now as signs of decline, now as manifestations of a new ascending life, of higher culture.

Such is, for example, his attitude to conscious life. The development of consciousness is always bound up with the intensified development of the nervous system: heightened cerebral activity usually goes at the expense of muscular development. Being the instrument of communication between men, consciousness simultaneously strengthens the need for such communication. To live consciously means to live in an atmosphere familiar to all men. On this basis, Nietzsche sees in consciousness the manifestation of the herd principle. "In the end," he says, "growing consciousness is a danger: whoever lives among conscious Europeans understands that it is a disease."[288] On the other hand, in Nietzsche's eyes, the highest consciousness is the seal of genius, that which elevates the individual above the state of degeneration and decline. Consciousness thus appears for our philosopher now as a sign of dependence and weakness, now as an expression of surplus strength and superiority: on the one hand, it raises man to the dignity of personality; on the other, it is precisely that which deprives him of personality.

The opposites of decline and elevation of life correspond in Nietzsche, as we have seen, to the opposition of aristocracy and democracy. It is not difficult to see that here too we are dealing with concepts essentially contradictory and ambiguous. Democracy for our writer appears now as synonymous with nervous weakness, flaccidity, physiological degeneration in general, now as synonymous with intellectual nullity. In the same way, aristocracy means now the superiority of a race stronger in nerves and muscles, now the superiority of men exceptionally gifted. The very German word *vornehm*, which Nietzsche uses to designate all that is aristocratic – a word resistant to exact translation – is ambiguous in essence: it may mean noble descent, or any other superiority of man over man. The social type which serves Nietzsche as the measure for evaluating all existing forms of human intercourse combines in itself the opposite traits of racial aristocracy and of intellectual, cultural aristocracy. In his depiction, the "nobility of the future" unites the qualities of a predatory beast, devouring "lambs," with those of the sage, legislating by right of reason.

With this is bound in Nietzsche the duality of juridical concepts. The dominion of the aristocracy is justified by him through the demands of "true justice," while this "justice" is now identified with the right of force, now, on the contrary, opposed to it. When it is a matter of the exploitation of the lower by the higher, Nietzsche finds it just, because it is natural: it is the result of physiological necessity. Here, then, the right of the stronger is acknowledged without limitation. But when the state devours the individual, when the mob overthrows the minority of masters by right of force, this provokes in Nietzsche indignation and disgust. Here, then, justice is understood as something opposed to force: "to equals the equal, to unequals the unequal – this is the true demand of justice."[289]

In short, in his judgments about human society, actual and ideal, Nietzsche stands now on the standpoint of pure naturalism, excluding moral evaluation, now on a normative, moral standpoint. The dominion of the nobility appears to him now as a fact destined to come in the future by irresistible natural necessity, now as an imperative norm, an ideal which man ought to follow. In his social doctrine Nietzsche wishes to stand beyond good and evil; yet he lays upon, if not all society, then at least the "higher men," a series of ethical demands: they ought not to content themselves with the role of cogs in the social machine; they ought not to sacrifice intellectual interests to material interests; they ought not to be ashamed of their dominion over the lower; they ought not to give themselves over to narrow specialization: they ought to strive for the all-round harmonious development of all their powers and abilities.

Nietzsche's social philosophy, like his philosophy as a whole, is at once a quest and a denial of the higher meaning of human existence. On the one hand, his entire protest against what he calls "democracy" and "degeneration" rests on the assumption that the goal of humanity is not satiety, not universal contentment: no material well-being can compensate man for the loss of those spiritual goods which condition his dignity as personality, which constitute his advantage over animals. On the other hand, it turns out that there is no goal capable of elevating man above the animal world. Blind force, the purposeless, aimless will to power, is the highest and the absolute in the world. Man is one of the manifestations of this blind element; therefore, the highest accessible to him is the maximum of power, the maximum of exploitation, the maximum of dominion over others. The gulf between man and animal, which was meant to be erected, disappears again, and the higher man proves to be in the highest degree an animal, the most terrible and cruel specimen of animal. And the lower must be content with the more modest role of domestic animals, instruments of the overman.

CHAPTER: XXIII

The Doctrine of the Overman

We have reached Nietzsche's central idea. For him, the thought of the "overman" embodies the justification of his life and the entire meaning of his philosophizing. Let us look more closely at this thought.

First of all, note its closest connection with the teaching already outlined above concerning the purposelessness of all that exists. There is no goal in the world, no meaning; yet all human life is built on the assumption of some final goal that justifies existence. It follows that this representation of a "goal" is nothing more than the expression of human caprice and arbitrariness. Individuals and entire peoples set themselves goals according to their own judgment and taste. "Up to now," says Zarathustra, "there have been thousands of goals, for there have been thousands of peoples. But as yet there are no chains binding these thousands together: there is no single goal. Humanity still has no goal. But tell me, my brothers, if humanity still has no goal, does it not mean that as yet there is no humanity itself?"[290]

A being without a goal is thereby petty, insignificant, and unworthy of the name man. If all those ends which humanity has set itself up to now have proved illusory, then a new goal must be set before man. But moral outlooks, false at their foundation, have not saved the person from insignificance. The collapse of morality, immediately impending, must bring with it further disintegration in society, further diminishment, and downfall of the individual. Therefore, humanity needs a new goal and a new love more than ever. The destruction of man must be halted by a new act of creation.[291]

In this sense, Zarathustra addresses the people: "The time

has come for man to set his goal before himself. The time has come for man to plant the seed of his highest hope. Even now, the soil is fertile enough for it. But one day it will become barren, meager, and no high tree will be able to grow in it." "Alas, the time approaches when humanity will no longer be able to bring forth from itself any star! Alas, the time approaches of the most despicable man, who will no longer be able to despise himself!"[292]

The new goal Nietzsche wants to set before man is nothing transcendent to man himself, for above man there is no other, higher reality. If there is no God above man, it means that man himself must become for himself the highest, the divine. The single God must be replaced by a multiplicity of human gods; the death of God is at the same time the resurrection of polytheism. "The divine consists precisely in this: that there are gods, but no God."[293] But the deified man is at the same time the transfigured man, wholly different from the present dwarf-man: something must be born "that will surpass in greatness the storm, the mountains, and the sea, and yet be the son of man."[294]

The new goal for man can only be a new human, more precisely, a new superhuman type. "Listen, I proclaim to you the overman," says Zarathustra. "The overman is the meaning of the earth. Let your will say: let the overman be the meaning of the earth."[295] Once the overman becomes our highest goal, he fills with meaning not only the human world but also "the whole earth," that is, all of natural life; if the overman is for us the supreme value, then all that exists must be evaluated in relation to him. Our entire life must be adapted to this goal: we must work and invent in order to build the dwelling for the overman; we must prepare the earth, animals, and plants for him; for his sake, we must be willing to desire our own destruction.[296]

The "new goal" at once changes the illumination of all surrounding reality, of all our present and past. For man, it embodies his task and at the same time his justification. In the process of world evolution, each stage of organic life serves as a transition from the lower to the higher: all beings up to now have produced out of themselves something higher; in man, this upward movement of life must continue: he too must bring forth from himself a higher form of existence – the overman. "What is the ape in relation to man? A laughingstock or a painful shame! The same must man be for the overman: a laughingstock or a painful shame. You have made your way from worm to man, and much in you is still worm. Once you were apes, and even now man is more of an ape than any ape!"[297]

Man is in all respects an intermediate link, "a rope stretched between animal and overman and suspended over an abyss." Outstanding and worthy of love in man is precisely that he is not the final goal, but only a bridge to the overman, a transitional and therefore perishable form of life.[298] Even the highest men of our time are nothing more than such bridges and transitions, fathers and forefathers of the overman yet to be born.[299] The transition to a better future shows itself in the disgust which the present inspires in higher men, in their despair and contempt for the present: for in this despair is revealed their longing "for other shores".[300]

What then must a man do who sees in himself only a preparatory stage for the future? He must devote to this future all his thought and will; he must not concern himself, along with the rest of men, about the longest possible preservation and greatest possible well-being of man; instead, he must see his essential task in Zarathustra's question: "how is man to be overcome?" The little virtue, petty worldly wisdom, paltry cares, antlike bustle, wretched contentment, and the "happiness of the majority" – all this the higher men must overcome![301]

The absence of a final goal in the world is equivalent to the absence of good and evil in it. But he who creates a goal for man thereby restores to the earth its meaning and its future. Only by this creative deed can man once again make good distinguishable from evil.³⁰² To create a goal means to bring meaning not only to the future. In creating out of human material the overman, we thereby also create a posthumous justification for all the dead; we give meaning and purpose to their lives and to all the past in general. We transform all that has been into the wished-for,³⁰³ into what ought to have been. At the same time, we give man the happiness of creation – the only happiness that has value: all men must take part in the creation of the overman and in this find their happiness.³⁰⁴

The "overman" embodies our new and higher love, the sole object worthy of our love and able to satisfy our need for it.³⁰⁵ Worthy of love is neither the present nor the past, but only the future: one must love not one's near ones but one's distant ones.³⁰⁶ We can love truly only our children, that better, higher humanity that is to be born from us. We want to create a new being, to take part in its birth, to love it, to bear it in our womb; in the overman, we have the goal for which we can love and respect one another: all other goals are worthy of destruction. In the overman, even our self-love finds its justification, for it is the sign of pregnancy: present-day humanity is big with the future; its sufferings are the pangs of birth.³⁰⁷

CHAPTER: XXIV

What then are those qualities of the overman that make him our goal? If he were a being wholly different from us, absolutely alien to us, we could form no conception of him. But from Nietzsche's point of view, the overman is a continuation of man. His qualities already lie latent within us; we can judge of him from the human material out of which he is to be formed. "When I created the overman," says Nietzsche, "I could not exclude from him anything human. All your malice and falseness, all your lies and ignorance, all this lies hidden in his seed."[308] The overman is "synthetic man" par excellence: his image results from the fusion into one whole of what is fragmentary and partial in individuals.[309] Yet in him there is no place for what in man appears petty and contemptible: he embodies the totality of all that is great in man, the ocean in which our contempt must be drowned.[310]

Looking more closely at those qualities in which Nietzsche sees the marks of greatness, the germs of superhumanity, we see that they are, for the most part, defined by negation of the average, ordinary man. The ordinary man is everywhere submissive to custom; by contrast, the great in man is always the "unusual," the "rare"; great is he who is unlike others. But since these "others," the human crowd, have in different historical epochs far from the same physiognomy, the marks of greatness are different at different times. In our own days, under the rule of the democratic ideal, the sign of greatness is aristocratism: great is he who does not go with the multitude, who withdraws from the crowd, who lives for himself and not for others, he who deviates from the everyday norm. If the distinguishing mark of the ordinary man is obedience to the prevailing morality, then the "great" man stands "beyond good and evil": he is "a criminal" by essence, for he breaks all existing tablets of values; his entire life is a continuous violation of the laws that govern the masses; the germ of the superhuman in him is above all his "malice." In opposition to "herd humanity," the great are "hermits," "lonely ones"; from them in time will grow the chosen people who will create the overman out of themselves.

In *Zarathustra*, Nietzsche depicts a series of types of the "higher men" of our time. They still bear the stamp of decline – the characteristic mark of all that is modern; yet at the same time, they already contain within themselves the germs of the overman to be born: they are his forerunners and forefathers. All of them are above all negators, fugitives, who have withdrawn from modern society, renounced modern beliefs, "men of great contempt and despair." First among them is Zarathustra himself, the most godless of the godless: he knows no equal, for he has rejected every law save his own will; every human society is to him an object of loathing; he saves himself from men in the solitude of his cave, situated on the highest mountain peak, amid snow and ice, among inaccessible rocks. He is the enemy of all compassion – he wants to be as hard as diamond; but he is still only a prophetic figure, a preparatory stage to the overman, for he has not yet overcome within himself his last sin, the last remnant of humanity – pity for the best, the "higher men."

To Zarathustra's cave come visitors – the "higher men" too, but standing a step below him: they seek instruction and demand help. The first is the soothsayer, "the preacher of the great weariness," type of the modern pessimist. He teaches that "all in the world is indifferent, every striving vain, the world has no meaning, knowledge weighs like a nightmare, seeking is barren, and there are no blessed isles." After him come kings, sated with power; they are nauseated at ruling over rabble, at being first among scum; it is repugnant to them to occupy a higher station without being by nature higher; in themselves and their subjects, they see only the type of degenerate man: they seek the higher man worthy to rule the earth. After the king comes "the conscientious scholar" – a man of learning, disillusioned with knowledge, his conscientiousness does not tolerate dilettantism: he wants knowledge absolutely specific, precise, and prefers to know nothing rather than know much by halves; and he is crushed by the paltriness of what is accessible to human knowing. He has devoted his life to studying the brain of the leech: this is his world, beyond which he knows nothing perfectly. Another type of higher man is the magician – an artist disillusioned with his art. He has the gift of charming, deceiving others, but he cannot deceive himself: before men he poses as a great enchanter, but he is himself oppressed by the sense of his nullity and the falsity of his art; everything in him is false; he is truthful only in his loathing of himself and of others, in his longing for the unattainable ideal of the great and truthful man.

Nietzsche next portrays "the last pope"; this priest lost his faith "out of piety," because his religious need found no satisfaction in his own religion; and so he wanders without task, without service, and without joy, stunned by the news of God's death. The same disillusion and grief confront us in the figure of "the ugliest of men" – "the murderer of God." For him, God was above all "the witness of human weakness" and, as it were, its embodiment. God saw all the depth of human ugliness and shame: his compassion penetrated everywhere, spared not human shame, and made man feel the whole abyss of his nothingness. "The ugliest of men" could not bear such a witness: he slew God; it was for him an act of vengeance.

The next visitor to Zarathustra is the voluntary beggar, one more of those rejected by society. He once possessed great wealth, but grew ashamed of his riches and was filled with disgust at the rich of today, that "gilded rabble" who would extract profit from any filth. Turning away from the rich, the "voluntary beggar" turned to the poor out of the fullness of his heart; but they too rejected him: they also proved to be "rabble," petty, envious men, rebellious slaves. He turned away from the poor and began to preach to cows.

The last visitor is Zarathustra's own shadow, the embodiment of all his negation and sorrow. "With you," says the shadow to him, "I strove toward all that is forbidden, worst, remotest: my only virtue is that I feared no prohibitions. With you, I broke all that my heart once revered; I cast aside all boundary-stones and images; I ran toward the most perilous desires, climbed above every crime. With you, I unlearned belief in words, values, and great names." This is a phantom that wanders without joy and without a goal, and Zarathustra flees from his dark shadow.

In the end, all those "higher men" who gather in Zarathustra's cave are united in negation; all are men who have despaired of God and of modern man: the expression of their everyday mood is the rite of "the ass-worship," a blasphemous parody of divine service which they all together perform in Zarathustra's cave. Negation in itself cannot be an ideal and a goal, and therefore Nietzsche is dissatisfied with his "higher men": they are only a preparatory stage and a foreshadowing of the coming generation of "overmen." Zarathustra awaits others, more powerful, victorious, beautiful in soul and body: they must be "laughing lions." Only such men can Zarathustra call his children and heirs. "You are not beautiful and noble enough for me," he says to the higher men. "I need pure, smooth mirrors for my teachings; on your surface, my own image is still distorted!"

Nietzsche tries to rise above negative definitions and fill the idea of the "overman" with positive content, but all these positive traits scatter like smoke at the first touch of analysis. At the base of the whole doctrine of the overman lies, in part, a denial prettified with images, and in part, a hopeless contradiction of incompatible aims.

The positive quality Nietzsche values first in the overman is strength: we saw that he recognizes the degree of power as the sole measure of value. From this point of view, it is clear that the whole value of the overman reduces solely to contrast with weaker people, with the mass, with the crowd. Yet we saw that the mass of men, from Nietzsche's standpoint, not only has no value, but on the contrary deserves contempt and loathing. If the "overman" is valuable only in comparison with what has no value, then obviously he himself is a merely imagined, spurious value. From a cosmic point of view, he is one of the most negligible phenomena, a grain of sand on the earth's crust that is a little higher than some other grains.

The whole significance of the overman reduces to contrast. In himself, he is nothing: to be something, he must rise above and flaunt over others; he needs a human pedestal, "the rabble" over which he can swagger, and spectators before whom he can pose. Is this the "meaning of the earth" and the "goal of human existence"?

Nietzsche himself dimly feels the falsity of his standpoint. For him, the "overman" is the highest form of existence. But what can "higher" and "lower" mean in a world where there is neither up nor down, where the very scale for determining the superiority of some forms over others is absent? Modern evolutionists depict the development of the organic world as a progressive movement, a transition from lower forms to higher. On this hypothesis rest Nietzsche's hopes for a possible transition of humanity to the higher type of the overman. But suddenly, he asks himself whether, at the base of the whole hypothesis of development, there does not lie a false and arbitrary hierarchy of values. Who told us that the passage from one form to another is a passage to the better and higher? In essence one could just as convincingly prove the opposite, i.e., that the entire process of world evolution, up to and including man, is continuous decline: man – and precisely the wisest man – is the extreme limit of nature's self-contradiction and error, for he is the most suffering being; the organic world itself is a product of the degeneration of the inorganic.[311]

To stand "beyond good and evil," as Nietzsche wants, means to renounce all values: from this point of view, one man is not higher or more valuable than another, for all men, like all phenomena of nature in general, are equally valueless. If so, there can be no talk of an "overman." Meanwhile, the "overman" is the central concept of Nietzsche's philosophy: he is precisely what lends beauty, meaning, and appeal to the whole picture of world life. How, then, did this transformation of the indifferent into the beautiful and valuable occur?

Nietzsche himself disclosed his secret in the following poetic image.

"This mountain gives beauty and meaning to the entire landscape over which it rules. Having said this to ourselves for the hundredth time, we show our imprudence and ingratitude by thinking that it itself, the source of this enchantment, must be the most enchanting part of the landscape; we make the ascent and experience disappointment. Suddenly, the magic that adorned both the mountain and the landscape vanishes for us! We forgot that much that is good and great appears so only at a certain distance, and indeed from below, not from above – only under this condition can it act upon us. Perhaps among those around you, you know people who must look at themselves from a certain distance in order to find themselves at all tolerable or attractive and strengthening."[312]

In these lines, written two years before *Zarathustra*, Nietzsche did not have the "overman" in mind; and yet they contain the whole secret of the latter. If you look at him from above, he is exposed in all his emptiness and lack of content. To see in him the "beauty and meaning of life," you must look from below, at a certain remove and through an artificial perspective. The "overman" is a nerve-jangling, showy spectacle, but it is easy to see that the whole effect is achieved by optical deception.

The general sense of a whole series of definitions of the

"overman" reduces to the negation of man and humanity. Recognizing in Napoleon I the embodiment of his ideal, Nietzsche says outright that he was "a synthesis of overman and nonman".[313] The combination of such qualities as extraordinary power and extraordinary inhumanity makes him see an "overman" also in Cesare Borgia.[314] What, one asks, can be attractive in a predatory man, an exploiter, cruel, knowing no pity? Inhumanity as such can only inspire disgust; but in specific surroundings it can produce a kind of theatrical effect: by contrast with petty pilferers and herd animals in human shape, the large predator can seem a lion; cruelty, if constantly juxtaposed with flaccidity, nervous weakness, and effeminacy, will in the end pass for "diamond hardness"; pitilessness will sooner or later be taken for "strength of will," a brazen brow for noble metal, and fine words for philosophy. Nietzsche himself says: *un monstre gai vaut mieux qu'un sentimental ennuyeux*[315] (a happy monster is worth more than a sentimental bore).

Nietzsche's philosophy is a protest against the trivialization and degeneration of modern man, but in this very degeneration lies one source of its colossal popularity. We are bored by the "gloomy people" passing before us in endless file. Our nerves are tired of the monotonous picture of the vulgarity surrounding us, and our degenerate taste craves intense sensations. The "overman" provided a spectacle that amused us and seemed for a time to fill one of the gaps of our existence. But now we have been amused enough, and it is time to tear off his mask.

One of Nietzsche's fundamental theses is that there is nothing in the world valuable in itself. The absence of absolute values must be made good by creation; otherwise, life becomes unbearable.[316] From Nietzsche's own standpoint, the "overman" is nothing more than a poetic fiction, a fabricated value, invented to adorn life. His Zarathustra says he could not reconcile himself to human existence if man were not a poet and a diviner.[317] But poetry, for Nietzsche, is an atmosphere of falsehood;

all poets lie, for they bring into the world a non-existent beauty; as a poet, Zarathustra himself lies. "Truly," he says, "we (poets) are ever drawn upward – into the realm of clouds; upon clouds we seat our motley dummies and then call them gods and overmen. They are just light enough for those chairs, all those gods and overmen." And a little further: "I am weary of poets".[318] Nietzsche speaks of the 'religious or half-religious' superstition that attributes superhuman qualities to genius; he deems it partly useful for the masses but ruinous for the genius himself. From this, however, it does not follow that a differing attitude toward the 'overman' is the boundary between the 'middle' and the last period of our philosopher's work. The just-quoted text from *Zarathustra* shows that even here the preaching of the 'overman' coexists with a negative attitude toward him and even with mockery of him.

It seems complicated to mock more bitterly the cherished dream of Nietzsche, which for him embodied the meaning of his existence, and yet here we have his genuine utterance. Lacking the possibility of filling life with real content, he had only to seem, to pose before others, and to admire himself. His Zarathustra played for him the role of a mirror adorned with the image of his own person. In him Nietzsche wished to embody the ideal of his own greatness; but he himself unmasked this greatness: from him we learn that in the great man he sees "always only the actor of his ideal".[319] And indeed, in every word and every gesture of Zarathustra one feels that he is playing a role in which he himself believes poorly.

First of all, he is a creator, a teacher, and a lawgiver. We have already seen that, as creator, he does not believe in his own creation, for in the end it reduces to the making of illusions, lying phantoms of beauty, goodness, and greatness – in a word, fictitious values. He is a "teacher" who has nothing to teach, for he does not believe in truth: for him, every human judgment is a lie. "I no longer believe in anything," says Nietzsche, "such is the proper cast of mind of creative personalities".³²⁰ On this basis, Zarathustra laughs at those pupils who believe in him. "You say that you believe in Zarathustra," he proclaims to them. "But what is Zarathustra! You are my believers – but what can all believers amount to! You have not yet sought yourselves, and therefore you found me. Thus, all believers do, and therefore all belief means so little. Now I call upon you to lose me and find yourselves; and only then shall I return to you, when you all have forsworn me."³²¹ These words are not only a warning against faith in authority but a denial of teaching itself: Zarathustra has no truths to impart to his pupils.³²² He preaches the overman to them and urges them to seek him, but the "overman" for him is not truth, only a poetic dream.

Equally fictitious is Zarathustra's "legislation." We have already seen that Nietzsche's philosophy denies the possibility of any universal legislation, any prescriptions binding for all men. Accordingly, Zarathustra declares that his legislation is addressed not to all but only to some, not to the people but to the chosen. He does not seek a herd but companions to whom he can show the glow of the rainbow and all the steps toward overmanhood.³²³ However, as we have seen, in *Zarathustra* and other works of Nietzsche, there are many passages where the "overman" appears as a single goal which all men must serve, partly as material, partly as instruments, conscious or blind. But this is one of those contradictions with which Nietzsche's doctrine abounds. Yet is any objective legislation possible, from Nietzsche's standpoint, even for the chosen? For the "chosen" are precisely those who acknowledge nothing obligatory for themselves, who deny the very idea of duty!

Legislation, according to Nietzsche, is a sign of dominion over others; but "to rule," he says, "is to impose my type. Why, that is dreadful! Isn't my happiness precisely in contemplating the multitude of other types?"³²⁴ In the end, the doctrine of the "overman" is individualism driven to the extreme, which excludes the possibility of binding the will of the individual by any rules. Therefore, all of Zarathustra's lawgiving stands, for Nietzsche himself, under a question mark. Unable to create a single code, he directly declares that "Zarathustra is a herald who summons many lawgivers."[325] But a multitude of lawgivers, each of whom legislates only for himself, in essence means the absence of any legislation whatsoever. Feeling this difficulty, Nietzsche makes, among other things, the following slip: the aim of legislation is to arouse the spirit of contradiction. "From me there must go forth a law, as though I wished to recreate all in my own image, so that in the struggle against me personality might come to know itself and be strengthened."[326] In the end, Nietzsche died with the question unresolved: "What meaning is there at all in issuing laws?"[327]

Above, we saw that, for Nietzsche, the image of the overman is obtained by fusing into one all that is great which exists in separate men. It now turns out that all the marks of human greatness have a fictitious character. One asks what kind of magnitude can result from the synthesis of a multitude of zeros!

Among the marks of superhumanity we have so far left one aside: cheerfulness, laughter, the joyousness of an existence that has overcome suffering and attained its highest goal. But even here Zarathustra shows himself first and foremost as the actor of his ideal. We have already had occasion to be convinced that cheerfulness in Nietzsche is a mask, a way of concealing suffering. Since the object of all this joy consists in fictitious values, an invented goal of life, the cheerfulness cannot help but be affected, theatrical. In Zarathustra's very laughter, one feels not joy but a bitter mockery of man and his philosophical quest, an attempt to make life ridiculous. This attempt, however, does not always succeed. "You have lost your goal," Zarathustra says to his shadow; "woe to you – how will you get over and laugh off this loss. For thereby you have lost your way." And immediately after that Zarathustra invites the shadow into the cave with the words: "This evening I shall have dances".[328]

We are already acquainted with the visitors who gather in this cave. In answer to the requests of all these sufferers, these men unsatisfied with life, Zarathustra proposes that they break into a dance. "Lift up your hearts, my brothers, and do not forget your legs. Give free rein to your legs, you skillful dancers, or better still – stand on your heads! This wreath of laughter, this wreath of roses, I myself set it on my head. In our day, no one but I proved strong enough for this!"[329]

Preaching love of life, Zarathustra is nevertheless himself convinced of the madness of this love: "In all love," he says, "there is madness; but in all madness there is a bit of reason. And to me, for all my inclination to life, it seems that butterflies, soap-bubbles, and all those people who are like them know best of all what happiness is."[330] Yet Zarathustra himself is not granted the butterfly's happiness, and laughter in him cannot overcome sadness. On a lovely summer evening, he delights in the dance of girls in a forest glade. But the dance ends, the girls depart, and sadness takes hold of him. "The sun set long ago," he said at last, "the meadow has grown damp, and coolness has breathed from the forests. Something unknown approaches me and looks at me with questions. What, are you still alive, Zarathustra? Why, for what, by what power, to what end, how! Is it not madness to continue life! My friends, it is the evening that raises these questions within me! Forgive me my sadness! It was evening – forgive me that it was evening."[331]

In these moments of sorrow, Nietzsche seems to forget his role: vanity gives way to sincerity, the mask of the overman falls off, and a sympathetic, human note sounds in his speech. In his sufferings, he is certainly no actor. But his whole inner life is a continual alternation of opposing states, a series of leaps from one extreme to the other. Struggling with the hopeless anguish that rises from the depths of his soul, he lives in a state of perpetual overstrain; the delirium of grandeur constantly gets the upper hand over the consciousness of his human frailty. His self-conceit knows no bounds. "I want to create things," he says, "against which time is powerless, to create for myself in form and in essence a little immortality; I have never been modest enough to dream of less." He calls his *Zarathustra* "the profoundest book humanity has ever possessed".[332] From the day of the "revaluation of all values," i.e., from the day of the appearance of his own doctrine, he proposes to begin a new reckoning of time.[333] His *alter ego* – Zarathustra – is surrounded by symbols of wisdom and power: above Zarathustra's head hovers the eagle, "the most proud of animals," and around the eagle's neck coils the serpent – "the wisest of animals".[334] To these heralds of wisdom is added the lion – a sign of the coming generation of "overmen," "the children of Zarathustra." It fawns upon Zarathustra and drives away from his cave the visitors, the flabby breed of the "higher men" of our time. In his doctrine, Nietzsche sees the beginning of a world crisis, a universal revolution, destined to come no later than 1890. "I am a fate for humanity," he writes to his friend Brandes a year before his madness.[335]

However, in lucid moments, Nietzsche judges himself more correctly. In the preface to the essay on Wagner, he writes, among other things: "I am just as much a son of my time as Wagner, that is, a decadent – with the difference that I understood this and rebelled against it."[336] To this judgment we too would subscribe.

CHAPTER: XXV

Conclusion

That Nietzsche's doctrine bears the mark of the decline of philosophical thought becomes evident as soon as we attempt to sum it up. In all his works, one feels a great philosophical and artistic talent. In individual aphorisms, we are struck by the depth with which philosophical problems are posed, by the subtlety of observation and critique, by the fireworks of wit, by the richness and vividness of imagery. But taken as a whole, Nietzsche's philosophy produces the impression of something extraordinarily disordered and shapeless: it amazes by its lack of logical unity and the poverty of its results.

What we find in it is an extraordinary motley, an anarchy of heterogeneous elements, uncoordinated with each other and not carried through to the end. Alongside an uncritical rejection of metaphysics, we find equally uncritical assertions about being – a naïve metaphysics resting on unconscious dogmatism; elements of positivism collide, in the very same works, with mockery of positivism and with a monistic doctrine of being. Nietzsche's theory of knowledge, which in fact is an outright denial of knowledge, is a conscious return to the pre-Socratic standpoint of the ancient sophists; at the same time, it completely overthrows all other parts of his own doctrine, for that doctrine everywhere applies, without scruple, the very categories of the intellect rejected by his epistemology. Further, in Nietzsche's moral teaching, we find, on the one hand, the same sophistry, the denial of any objective values and norms of conduct, and on the other hand, a teaching about an objective scale of values rooted in the very nature of being; and this scale turns out to be dual. In Nietzsche's social philosophy, we find individualism carried to an anarchic extreme, excluding the possibility of any legislation whatever, and alongside it faith in the philosopher-lawgiver of the future who will remake the social life of mankind on new foundations. Finally, in the image of the overman – half beast, half philosopher – we find, as it were, the sum of all the inner contradictions of Nietzsche's doctrine and outlook.

In the end, Nietzsche's philosophy ceases to speak the human tongue and begins to roar like a beast: Zarathustra's last response to the philosophical demands of modern humanity is the roar of a lion that scatters all seekers and questioners. It seems hardly possible to go further along the path of the brutalization and degeneration of thought. And yet, as a "sign of the future," this prophetic lion shows what we may still expect from the "children" of Zarathustra.

We have already more than once pointed out the importance of the fundamental task Nietzsche set himself, as well as the depth and seriousness of his intellectual striving. Yet the final conclusions of his philosophy verge on the banal! How is this colossal disproportion to be explained – between the forces expended and the results attained? The very extraordinariness of Nietzsche's gifts proves that his failure is due chiefly to causes not depending on him personally. In this failure is reflected the general weakening and exhaustion of thought, which is the characteristic mark of our entire epoch.

In the intellectual atmosphere we breathe, there is something that cuts the wings of philosophy. In the days of the highest flourishing of philosophy, it was animated by faith in reason, by faith in thought as the foundation of existence. In the epoch of ancient philosophy's bloom, Socrates defined being as a concept, Plato saw in it the idea, Aristotle believed in the form of forms, the all-embracing world reason. In the days of classical German philosophy, Kant taught that the intellect is the lawgiver of nature, that the whole world of phenomena is conditioned by the forms of thought; Fichte understood the universe as the revelation of the absolute "I"; Schelling and Hegel attempted to comprehend the world-process as the development of the "absolute spirit."

For the greatest thinkers of antiquity and of modern times, to believe in thought meant to recognize in it not merely our subjective state but the objective determination of being. We have already seen that this is the presupposition not only of all philosophy but of all knowledge in general, indeed of every act of consciousness. If being were absolutely alien to thought, it would not only be absolutely unknowable, it could not even appear to us; for whatever appears to us thereby becomes thought, reveals itself as thought. If thought were only our subjective state, if it did not express the objective reality of being, then it would, by that very fact, be a phantom without real content: we could not know either being or phenomena. In the end, knowledge rests on the presupposition that thought is the universal, all-embracing form of existence.

This presupposition cannot be proved, for it lies at the foundation of our consciousness, conditions every act of our thinking, and therefore every proof as well: before proving anything whatever we already presuppose the universality and necessity of the forms of thought, the applicability of these forms to being; every proof already proceeds from the assumption that thought can serve as the expression of being and that, accordingly, it constitutes its determination.

Closely bound up with faith in thought as universal and all-embracing is another presupposition of our consciousness, equally necessary and equally indemonstrable: the presupposition of a universal and all-embracing goal lying at the foundation of all existence. Our whole consciousness and our whole life appear as a series of goals, and the variety of separate manifestations of our consciousness and our activity corresponds to the multiplicity of goals we pursue. But all this diversity of goals presupposes, as has already been said, a single absolute goal, for the sake of which it is worth living, acting, and thinking at all – a goal desirable in itself and not for the sake of something else. Otherwise, everything in our life is purposeless, illogical, senseless: all in it is false and all our reason is an illusion. This goal cannot be the product, the result of our thought, for it conditions all thought. For the same reason, it cannot be proved by us, for every proof already presupposes that there is such an absolute goal for the sake of which it is worth thinking and proving at all. In short, at the foundation of our consciousness lies the presupposition of such a goal as is not conditioned but, on the contrary, conditions and justifies ourselves – the presupposition of a universal, all-embracing goal.

Greatness can be achieved only by that philosophy which believes in its own presuppositions, in those necessary postulates which condition all consciousness whatever. Renouncing that by which every living thought lives, that which reason breathes, philosophy renounces itself, condemns itself to inevitable degeneration.

This is precisely what we observe in the chief currents of philosophical thought of the second half of the nineteenth century. For all their diversity, the most popular doctrines of the epoch – pessimism, materialism, and positivism – converge in a common disbelief in thought, in a typical reaction against the idealism that had earlier prevailed. At the root of Schopenhauer's pessimism lies the irreconcilable dualism of the world as will and the world as representation. The entire world of representations is false, an illusion; being is absolutely alien to thought, in its essence irrational, senseless, and purposeless. From the standpoint of materialism, likewise, all existence is the manifestation of a meaningless, irrational force; thought itself is no more than a particular expression of blind elemental energy, a function of the brain. Similarly, the teaching of positivists and agnostics of various shades concerning the unknowability of being means, in the end, that being is absolutely alien to thought. At a further stage of its development, this standpoint must pass into complete illusionism. Whoever rejects the knowability of being, if consistent, must finally reject the knowability of the phenomena of being as well. As we have seen, Nietzsche in fact reached this result, denying the very concept of phenomenon.

Having lost faith in reason, philosophy was bound to despair of man as well; for if reason – that which distinguishes man from the animal – is a lie, then nothing remains to justify faith in human dignity. Nietzsche's sophistic teaching represents the completion of the decline of modern philosophical thought, and let us hope for its extreme limit. But this teaching, like many others, merely gives theoretical form to what society as a whole is experiencing – its intellectual strivings, longings, and hopes. The decline of philosophy reflects the general decline of contemporary humanity.

That in our day personality has become depersonalized, tastes have degenerated, interests have shrunk, and creativity has dried up – this cannot be doubted. Nietzsche observed the phenomenon correctly, but he was unable to give it any satisfactory explanation. It is obvious above all that the degeneration of personality cannot be explained by the democratization of modern society. Did democracy engender the "Americanism" that has seized the modern world? Is democracy to blame for the predominance of material interests over intellectual ones? Rather the opposite: the passion for gain is bound up with unrestricted competition, with inequality of fortunes, with the limitless possibility of amassing wealth and concentrating it in a few hands; it is the inevitable accompaniment of the capitalist system. If the modern worker plays the role of a wheel, a cog in the social machine, this again is not the fault of democracy: quite the contrary, it is precisely the democratic movement of our time that aims to secure for the worker "human conditions of existence," to shorten his working hours, to give him leisure for intellectual activity, self-development, and self-education. Nineteenth-century labor legislation has already done much to set limits to the exploitation of labor and to mitigate the "impersonal slavery" of the working class.

The depersonalization of personality lies not in democracy as such; on the contrary, the democratic movement contains a strongly marked element of individualism; in it is expressed the striving of personality to become independent, to free itself from class bondage. On the other hand, it is beyond doubt that democratic institutions in themselves, nor any social reforms whatever, can save personality from degeneration and diminishment: the latter depends not only on external conditions, and therefore not on the social order alone. A man for whom material means and conditions of life take the place of its goal is possible under any social system; and under any social system, such a man will be petty and base. Man rises above the herd principle, frees himself from the yoke of vulgarity, only when he places the center of his life not in what perishes, not in what lives for one day, but in the eternal and the unconditional.

The root of decline lies in man's loss of that goal which lifts him above the sphere of the material and everyday, and sets the boundary between him and the animal.

Nietzsche's philosophy shows us better than anything what this loss means. The whole of it is a denial of the meaning of life and at the same time an unceasing anxiety and torment of seeking, a struggle between despair of man and the need for hope, between denial of reason and belief in reason. In Nietzsche's positive constructions, we find a series of weak, distorted reflections of that very thing he denies: the concept of goal, of value, of the ideal of the rational, the "true" man. All this, by his own admission, is a shadow of God. And it turns out that he cannot take a step without these shadows. His thought is bound to the very thing he denies. The God rejected nevertheless remains the center of his philosophy, and in this lies the religiosity of his quest.

In countless writings, Nietzsche repeats in every key: "God is dead, God is dead": he says it through the mouths of the "madman," Zarathustra, the former pope, and many times in his own person. The result of these endless repetitions is the impression that Nietzsche wants to rid himself of a haunting nightmare, to persuade himself and others that this is only a delusion and not reality. But all his efforts are in vain: he denies that which he lives by.

In the end, we must recognize that for Nietzsche, there is no small merit. His entire philosophy is an extraordinarily eloquent testimony to the power and vitality of that very religious idea which he preaches against. If religious presuppositions underlie our entire life and activity, our faith in progress, and the ideals – ethical and social – that flow from it, does this not mean that these presuppositions are something indelible, inseparable from man? Only faith in the meaning of life gives us the strength to live. And so long as we live, denial does not penetrate to the depths, but remains on the surface of our consciousness.

Nietzsche wished to proclaim to humanity a new source of hope and joy. His whole philosophy is an attempt to overcome despair, to rise above the pessimism to which the logic of his thought irresistibly led him. Did this attempt succeed? Did he reach the goal of his wanderings? We have seen that he suffered a shipwreck, and he himself says of himself: "I am the eternal Jew, with the only difference that I am neither Jew nor eternal."

In one of his classic aphorisms, Nietzsche says, among other things: "Our sun has already set, and though we no longer see it, the sky of our life still shines above us, still glows with its afterglow." In these words seems contained the key to the riddle of modern man, which Nietzsche strove to solve: our faith in good, in man and his reason, all our values – all this is the afterglow of the sun that has now for a time set, but once shone brightly above us.

If these values do not die, if they continue to rule our thought and our will, this proves that, contrary to Nietzsche, we have not yet torn our earth from its sun, that within us still lives the eternal source of our hope. And if so, pessimism loses its mortal sting. We may await a new dawn; we need not fear the darkness of eternal night.

Citations

In the citations, the titles are written in German, exactly as in Trubetskoy's original text. This has been done to avoid confusion, since in English editions the references may not necessarily appear on the same page as in the original works. It must also be taken into account that the references are to the editions published before 1903, that is, before this book was written.

1. Jenseits von Gut und Böse, § 282. Bd. VII. S. 264. Quoted from the 1899 edition.
2. Der Wille zur Macht, § 38, Bd. VIII. S. 263.
3. Ibid., § 375. Bd. XV. S. 403.
4. Ibid., § 38. Bd. VIII. S. 263.
5. Zur Genealogie der Moral, § 12. Bd. VII. S. 325.
6. Also sprach Zarathustra. Bd. VI. S. 13.
7. Jenseits von Gut und Böse, § 227. Bd. VII. S. 182.
8. Die fröhliche Wissenschaft, § 307. Bd. V. S. 236.
9. Zur Genealogie der Moral, § 24. Bd. VII. S. 394.
10. Die fröhliche Wissenschaft, § 156. Bd. V. S. 182.
11. Die fröhliche Wissenschaft, § 316. Bd. V. S. 241.
12. On this division into periods see: Riehl. Friedrich Nietzsche, der Künstler und der Denker; Vaihinger. Nietzsche als Philosoph. S. 44 ff.; Gast Peter. Einführung in den Gedankengang von "Also sprach Zarathustra" // Nietzsche. Bd. VI. S. 4861.
13. Menschliches, Allzumenschliches, § 34. Bd. II. S. 51.
14. Nietzsche. Bd. VI. S. 489.
15. Die fröhliche Wissenschaft, § 324. Bd. V. S. 245; cf. § 10. S. 151–152.
16. Menschliches, Allzumenschliches, § 31, 32. Bd. II. S. 48–49.
17. See e.g. § 9, 16, 18, 32. Bd. II. S. 23–24, 32, 34–36, 49.
18. Der Wille zur Macht, § 460. Bd. XV. S. 469.
19. Bd. IX. S. 369.
20. Schopenhauer als Erzieher. Bd. I. S. 402.
21. Ibid. S. 430–431.
22. David Strauss, der Bekenner und der Schriftsteller. Bd. I. S. 229–231.
23. Schopenhauer als Erzieher. Bd. I. S. 430–431.
24. Ibid.
25. Schopenhauer als Erzieher. Bd. I. S. 428.
26. Richard Wagner in Bayreuth. Bd. I. S. 514.
27. Vom Nutzen und Nachtheil der Historie für das Leben. Bd. I. S. 291–292.

28. Richard Wagner in Bayreuth. Bd. I. S. 514.
29. Schopenhauer als Erzieher. Bd. I. S. 435–436; Vom Nutzen und Nachtheil der Historie. Bd. I. S. 285.
30. Schopenhauer als Erzieher. Bd. I. S. 445–446.
31. Ibid. S. 434, 438.
32. Schopenhauer als Erzieher. Bd. I. S. 438–445; Vom Nutzen und Nachtheil der Historie. Bd. I. S. 319, 322, 364, 367.
33. Schopenhauer als Erzieher. Bd. I. S. 491.
34. Ibid. S. 440.
35. Der Philosoph. Bd. X. S. 210.
36. Ibid. S. 211.
37. Vom Nutzen und Nachtheil der Historie. Bd. I. S. 366.
38. Die Geburt der Tragödie. Bd. I. S. 55.
39. Richard Wagner in Bayreuth. Bd. I. S. 523.
40. Die Geburt der Tragödie. Bd. I, esp. S. 31–32.
41. Ibid., S. 116.
42. Die Geburt der Tragödie. Bd. I. S. 116.
43. Richard Wagner in Bayreuth. Bd. I. S. 567.
44. Der Wille zur Macht, § 460. Bd. XV. S. 469; Der Fall Wagner, Vorwort. Bd. VIII. S. 1.
45. Der Fall Wagner, Vorwort. Bd. VIII. S. 2.
46. Der Wille zur Macht, § 460. Bd. XV. S. 470.
47. Aus der Zeit des Menschlichen, Allzumenschlichen. Bd. XI. S. 85.
48. Die fröhliche Wissenschaft, § 309. Bd. V. S. 237.
49. Ibid., § 124. Bd. V. S. 162.
50. Ibid., § 318. Bd. V. S. 242–243.
51. See the article by Mrs. Förster-Nietzsche in: Nietzsche's Werke. Bd. VI. S. 482–483.
52. Die fröhliche Wissenschaft, § 288. Bd. V. S. 217–218.
53. On this trait see the biography compiled by his sister Elisabeth Förster-Nietzsche: Bd. II. S. 47.
54. On this trait see the biography compiled by his sister Elisabeth Förster-Nietzsche: Bd. II. S. 47.
55. Schopenhauer als Erzieher. Bd. I. S. 429.
56. Die fröhliche Wissenschaft, § 183. Bd. V. S. 188.
57. Jenseits von Gut und Böse, § 279. Bd. VII. S. 262–263.
58. Der Wille zur Macht, § 286. Bd. XV. S. 296.
59. Die fröhliche Wissenschaft, § 312. Bd. V. S. 239–240.
60. Ibid., § 268. S. 204.
61. Ibid., § 325. S. 245–246.

62. Die fröhliche Wissenschaft, § 153. Bd. V. S. 181.
63. Ibid., § 287. S. 217.
64. Ibid., § 310. S. 237–238.
65. Götzendämmerung, Moral als Wiedernatur, § 3. Bd. VIII. S. 87.
66. Der Wille zur Macht, § 55. Bd. VIII. S. 295–296.
67. Jenseits von Gut und Böse, § 63. Bd. VII. S. 92.
68. Der Wille zur Macht, § 233. Bd. XV. S. 234.
69. Morgenröthe, § 423. Bd. IV. S. 291–292.
70. Jenseits von Gut und Böse, § 294. Bd. VII. S. 274.
71. Ibid., § 277. Bd. VII. S. 262.
72. Ibid., § 270. S. 259.
73. Ibid., § 40. S. 61.
74. Ibid., § 290. S. 268.
75. Ibid., § 40, 289. S. 61–62, 268.
76. Ibid., § 278. Bd. VII. S. 262.
77. Ibid., § 270. S. 258–259.
78. Ibid., § 273. Bd. VII. S. 270.
79. Also sprach Zarathustra. Bd. VI. S. 257.
80. Jenseits von Gut und Böse, § 273. Bd. VII. S. 260.
81. Also sprach Zarathustra. Bd. VI. S. 177.
82. Ibid. S. 246.
83. Ibid. S. 269.
84. Ibid. S. 210.
85. Die fröhliche Wissenschaft, § 278. Bd. V. S. 211–212.
86. Ibid., § 109. Bd. V. S. 147–149.
87. Götzendämmerung, Die Verbesserer der Menschheit, § 1, Bd. VIII. S. 104.
88. See for all the above: Die fröhliche Wissenschaft, § 109. S. 322, 1; Bd. VII. S. 147–149, 234–235, 33–37; Der Wille zur Macht, § 14. Bd. VIII. S. 229; Der Wille zur Macht. Bd. XV. § 384, 461, 173. S. 408, 471, 174–175; Der Wille zur Macht, §316, 323. Bd. XV. S. 332, 344–345.
89. For all the above on eternal recurrence, see: Die ewige Wiederkunft. Bd. XII. S. 51–69; Der Wille zur Macht. Bd. XV. § 375–381, 323. S. 403–412, 338, 344–345; Nachträge zum Zarathustra, § 719–731. Bd. XII. S. 369–371; Die fröhliche Wissenschaft, § 341. Bd. V. S. 265–266.
90. Die ewige Wiederkunft, § 104. Bd. XII. S. 57.
91. Ibid., § 120. Bd. XII. S. 65.
92. Nachträge zum Zarathustra, § 721. Bd. XII. S. 369.
93. Ibid., § 729, 730. Bd. XII. S. 370–371.
94. Die fröhliche Wissenschaft, § 1. Bd. V. S. 37.

95. Ibid. S. 33–37.
96. Die fröhliche Wissenschaft, § 125. Bd. V. S. 163–164.
97. Ibid., § 320. S. 244.
98. Versuch einer Selbstkritik. Bd. I. S. 13–14.
99. Menschliches, Allzumenschliches, § 28. Bd. II. S. 46; Der Wille zur Macht, § 59. Bd. XV. S. 14–19.
100. Der Wille zur Macht, § 280. Bd. XV. S. 288; Götzendämmerung. Bd. VIII. S. 90; Also sprach Zarathustra. Bd. VI. S. 240–244.
101. Der Wille zur Macht, § 461. Bd. XV. S. 471–472.
102. Also sprach Zarathustra. Bd. VI. S. 242; Der Wille zur Macht. Bd. XV. § 362, 365, 366, 374; S. 387, 399, 390–392.
103. Der Wille zur Macht, § 385, 480; Bd. XV. S. 411, 485–486.
104. Ibid., § 461. S. 471–472; Jenseits von Gut und Böse, § 56. Bd. VII. S. 80.
105. Der Wille zur Macht, § 478. Bd. XV. S. 484.
106. Die fröhliche Wissenschaft, § 107, 299, Bd. V. S. 142–143, 228–229.
107. Ibid., § 373. S. 330–331; Die ewige Wiederkunft, § 116, 117, 121, 124, 125. S. 64–67; Nachträge zum Zarathustra, § 723. S. 369–370.
108. Ibid., § 431, 371.
109. Der Wille zur Macht, § 375. Bd. XV. S. 403.
110. Die ewige Wiederkunft, § 151, 121. Bd. XII. S. 63, 65–66.
111. Der Wille zur Macht, § 376. Bd. XV. S. 403.
112. Götzendämmerung. Bd. VIII. S. 88–90, 100–101.
113. Jenseits von Gut und Böse, § 203. Bd. VII. S. 137–139.
114. Götzendämmerung. Bd. VIII. S. 161.
115. Morgenröthe, § 108. Bd. IV. S. 103; Menschliches, Allzumenschliches, § 34. Bd. II. S. 51–52.
116. Morgenröthe, Vorrede, § 4. Bd. IV, S. 8; Jenseits von Gut und Böse, § 226. Bd. VII. S. 181–182.
117. Menschliches, Allzumenschliches, § 33. Bd. II. S. 50–51; Der Wille zur Macht, § 383. Bd. XV. S. 408.
118. Menschliches, Allzumenschliches, § 33. Bd. II. S. 51.
119. Die fröhliche Wissenschaft, § 152. Bd. V. S. 180.
120. Jenseits von Gut und Böse, § 157. Bd. VII. S. 107.
121. Götzendämmerung. Bd. VIII. S. 131.
122. Die fröhliche Wissenschaft, § 276. Bd. V. S. 209.
123. Morgenröthe, § 124. Bd. IV. S. 125.
124. Die fröhliche Wissenschaft, § 11. Bd. V. S. 152.
125. Ibid., § 285. Bd. V. S. 216.
126. Die fröhliche Wissenschaft, § 2. Bd. V. S. 38.

127. Ibid., § 343. S. 272.
128. Ibid., § 324. S. 245.
129. Morgenröthe, § 429. Bd. IV. S. 296–297.
130. Also sprach Zarathustra. Bd. VI. S. 243.
131. Der Wille zur Macht, § 315. Bd. XV. S. 336–338.
132. Die fröhliche Wissenschaft, § 111. Bd. V. S. 152–153.
133. Menschliches, Allzumenschliches, § 31, 32. Bd. II. S. 48–49.
134. Die fröhliche Wissenschaft, § 265. Bd. V. S. 204.
135. Der Wille zur Macht, § 269, 270, 283–285. Bd. XV. S. 274–275, 291–294; Die fröhliche Wissenschaft, § 111. Bd. V. S. 152–153.
136. Der Wille zur Macht, § 269, 270. Bd. XV. S. 274–275.
137. Menschliches, Allzumenschliches, § 2. Bd. II. S. 18–19.
138. Ibid., § 32, 49.
139. Götzendämmerung. Bd. VIII. S. 77; see also S. 83; Der Wille zur Macht, § 279. Bd. XV. S. 286.
140. Menschliches, Allzumenschliches, § 20, 27. Bd. II. S. 37–38, 45.
141. Ibid., § 17, 33.
142. Der Wille zur Macht, § 279. Bd. XV. S. 286.
143. Götzendämmerung. Bd. VIII. S. 83.
144. Der Wille zur Macht, § 283–285. Bd. XV. S. 291–294; Götzendämmerung. Bd. VIII. S. 77.
145. Der Wille zur Macht, § 260. Bd. XV. S. 265; cf. Jenseits von Gut und Böse, § 17. S. 27.
146. Der Wille zur Macht, § 280. Bd. XV. S. 286; Die fröhliche Wissenschaft, § 112. Bd. V. S. 153–154.
147. Götzendämmerung. Bd. VIII. S. 93–94; Der Wille zur Macht, § 296, 298, 280. Bd. XV. S. 313–316, 318–320, 286–287; Die fröhliche Wissenschaft, § 127. Bd. V. S. 165.
148. Der Wille zur Macht, § 271. Bd. XV. S. 276.
149. Die fröhliche Wissenschaft, § 246. Bd. V. S. 200.
150. Jenseits von Gut und Böse, § 3. Bd. VII. S. 11–12.
151. Die fröhliche Wissenschaft, Preface, § 2. Bd. V. S. 7.
152. Der Wille zur Macht, § 233. Bd. XV. S. 234.
153. Ibid.
154. Ibid., § 237, 240. S. 239, 242.
155. Jenseits von Gut und Böse, Vorrede, Bd. VII. S. 3.
156. Der Wille zur Macht, § 317. Bd. XV. S. 339.
157. See generally Der Wille zur Macht, § 296–324. Bd. XV. S. 313–347, especially §§ 316, 317, 339; cf. Jenseits von Gut und Böse, § 186. Bd. VII. S. 115.

158. Der Wille zur Macht, § 279. Bd. XV. S. 286.
159. Jenseits von Gut und Böse, § 14. Bd. VII. S. 24; cf. § 204. S. 143–146.
160. Jenseits von Gut und Böse, § 6. Bd. VII. S. 14–15.
161. Morgenröthe, § 106. Bd. IV. S. 100–101.
162. Ibid.
163. Jenseits von Gut und Böse, § 221. Bd. VII. S. 174–175; Der Wille zur Macht, § 11. Bd. VIII. S. 226.
164. Also sprach Zarathustra. Bd. VI. S. 286.
165. Götzendämmerung. Bd. VIII. S. 102.
166. Jenseits von Gut und Böse, § 32. Bd. VII. S. 52–53.
167. Götzendämmerung. Bd. VIII. S. 120.
168. Morgenröthe, § 132. Bd. IV. S. 133–135.
169. Friedrich Nietzsche in seinen Werken, S. 130.
170. Cf. Zur Genealogie der Moral, §§ 4, 5. Bd. VII. S. 291–293.
171. Menschliches, Allzumenschliches, § 103. Vol. II, S. 103–106; Morgenröthe, § 133. Vol. IV, S. 135–138.
172. Die fröhliche Wissenschaft, § 338. Vol. V, S. 260.
173. Jenseits von Gut und Böse, § 30. Vol. VII, S. 49–50.
174. Morgenröthe, § 134, 137. Vol. IV, S. 138–139, 141.
175. Der Wille zur Macht, § 7. Vol. VIII, S. 221–223.
176. Götzendämmerung, Vol. VIII, S. 146–147.
177. Die fröhliche Wissenschaft, § 116. Bd. V. S. 156.
178. Der Wille zur Macht, Bd. VIII. S. 220–221.
179. Die fröhliche Wissenschaft, § 21. Bd. V. S. 58–59.
180. Menschliches, Allzumenschliches, § 89. Bd. III. S. 49
181. Jenseits von Gut und Böse, §§ 23, 44. S. 36, 65.
182. Die fröhliche Wissenschaft, § 19. Bd. V. S. 57.
183. Die fröhliche Wissenschaft, § 4. Bd. V. S. 41–42.
184. Morgenröthe, § 9. Bd. IV. S. 16.
185. Jenseits von Gut und Böse, § 116. Bd. VII. S. 101.
186. Der Wille zur Macht, § 428. Bd. XV. S. 447.
187. Jenseits von Gut und Böse, § 225. Bd. VII. S. 180–181.
188. Morgenröthe, § 174. Bd. IV. S. 170–171.
189. Jenseits von Gut und Böse, § 201. Bd. VII. S. 132–134.
190. Ibid., § 202. S. 135.
191. Ibid., § 52. S. 77.
192. Zur Genealogie der Moral, § 7. Bd. VII. S. 328.
193. Jenseits von Gut und Böse, § 267. Bd. VII. S. 253.
194. Die fröhliche Wissenschaft, § 118. Bd. V. S. 157–158.
195. Zur Genealogie der Moral, § 17. Bd. VII. S. 338.

196. Zur Genealogie der Moral, § 11. Bd. VII. S. 322.
197. Zur Genealogie der Moral. Bd. VII. S. 239–243.
198. Menschliches, Allzumenschliches, § 45. Bd. II. S. 68–69.
199. Jenseits von Gut und Böse, § 186. Bd. VII. S. 115.
200. Morgenröthe, § 174. Bd. IV. S. 171.
201. Jenseits von Gut und Böse, § 225. Bd. VII. S. 181.
202. Also sprach Zarathustra. Bd. VI. S. 305.
203. Jenseits von Gut und Böse, § 62. Bd. VII. S. 88–89.
204. Also sprach Zarathustra. Bd. VI. S. 130.
205. Ibid. S. 291.
206. Ibid. S. 312.
207. Der Wille zur Macht, § 462. Bd. XV. S. 472.
208. Ibid., § 10. S. 23.
209. Ibid., § 420. S. 440.
210. Der Wille zur Macht, § 353. Bd. XV. S. 368.
211. Götzendämmerung. Bd. VIII. S. 140; Der Wille zur Macht, § 227. Bd. XV. S. 225.
212. Götzendämmerung. Bd. VIII. S. 143.
213. Der Wille zur Macht, § 424. Bd. XV. S. 442–443.
214. Ibid., § 226. S. 224.
215. Ibid., § 86. S. 84.
216. Ibid., § 91, 332, 428. S. 96, 353, 447; Die fröhliche Wissenschaft, § 4. Bd. V. S. 41–42.
217. Götzendämmerung. Bd. VIII. S. 157–159.
218. Ibid.; cf.: Der Wille zur Macht, § 93, 331. Bd. XV. S. 96, 354.
219. Der Wille zur Macht, § 425. Bd. XV. S. 444.
220. Götzendämmerung. Bd. VIII. S. 145–146.
221. Der Wille zur Macht, § 143. Bd. XV. S. 138.
222. Ibid., § 428. S. 446.
223. Die fröhliche Wissenschaft, § 333. Bd. V. S. 252.
224. Zur Genealogie der Moral. Bd. VII. S. 338: "'Jenseits von Gut und Böse'... Dies heisst zum Mindesten nicht 'Jenseits von Gut und Schlecht'."
225. Jenseits von Gut und Böse, § 9. Bd. VII. S. 17.
226. Götzendämmerung. Bd. VIII. S. 88–89.
227. Ibid. S. 153–154.
228. Götzendämmerung. Bd. VIII. S. 108–109.
229. Die fröhliche Wissenschaft, § 111. Bd. V. S. 152–153.
230. Ibid., § 154. S. 181.
231. Ibid., § 307. S. 236.

232. Die fröhliche Wissenschaft, § 2, 319. Bd. V. S. 37–38, 243.
233. Der Wanderer und sein Schatten, § 350. Bd. III. S. 371.
234. Der Wille zur Macht, Bd. XV. S. 138.
235. Cf.: Also sprach Zarathustra. Bd. VI. S. 16, 418.
236. Götzendämmerung. Bd. VIII. S. 161–162.
237. Jenseits von Gut und Böse, § 257. Bd. VIII. S. 235.
238. Zur Genealogie der Moral. S. 436.
239. Jenseits von Gut und Böse, § 257. Bd. VII. S. 235–236.
240. Zur Genealogie der Moral. Bd. VII. S. 326.
241. Jenseits von Gut und Böse, § 259. Bd. VII. S. 238.
242. Jenseits von Gut und Böse, § 258. Bd. VII. S. 236–237.
243. Ibid., § 268. S. 255.
244. Götzendämmerung. Bd. VIII. S. 153.
245. Morgenröthe, § 206. Bd. IV. S. 203–205.
246. Ibid., § 173. S. 169–170.
247. Götzendämmerung. Bd. VIII. S. 153.
248. Die fröhliche Wissenschaft, § 129. Bd. V. S. 249–250.
249. Der Wille zur Macht, § 406. Bd. XV. S. 431–432.
250. Menschliches, Allzumenschliches, § 23. Bd. II. S. 40–41.
251. Jenseits von Gut und Böse, § 223. Bd. VII. S. 176.
252. Jenseits von Gut und Böse, § 215. Bd. VII. S. 170.
253. Morgenröthe, § 171. Bd. IV. S. 168.
254. Jenseits von Gut und Böse, § 224. Bd. VII. S. 176–179.
255. Götzendämmerung. Bd. VIII. S. 111.
256. Der Wille zur Macht, § 475. Bd. XV. S. 482.
257. Also sprach Zarathustra. Bd. VI. S. 204–205.
258. Die fröhliche Wissenschaft, § 366. Bd. V. S. 318–320.
259. Also sprach Zarathustra. Bd. VI. S. 184.
260. Jenseits von Gut und Böse, § 206. Bd. VII. S. 148–149.
261. Also sprach Zarathustra. Bd. VI. S. 183.
262. Jenseits von Gut und Böse, § 204. Bd. VII. S. 143–146.
263. Götzendämmerung. Bd. VIII. S. 148.
264. Genealogie der Moral. Bd. VII. S. 371–372.
265. Jenseits von Gut und Böse, § 22. Bd. VII. S. 35.
266. Götzendämmerung. Bd. VIII. S. 113.
267. Götzendämmerung. Bd. VIII. S. 111–112.
268. Also sprach Zarathustra. Bd. VI. S. 69–72.
269. Menschliches, Allzumenschliches, § 473. Bd. II. S. 350–351.
270. Götzendämmerung. Bd. VIII. S. 149–150.
271. Jenseits von Gut und Böse, § 202. Bd. VII. S. 136.

272. Ibid., § 44. Bd. VII. S. 64–65.
273. Götzendämmerung. Bd. VIII. S. 161–162.
274. Der Wille zur Macht, § 46. Bd. VIII. S. 280.
275. Götzendämmerung. Bd. VIII. S. 142.
276. Jenseits von Gut und Böse, § 199. Bd. VII. S. 130; cf. Nachträge zum Zarathustra, § 714. Bd. XII. S. 367; Die fröhliche Wissenschaft, § 174. Bd. V. S. 186.
277. Zur Genealogie der Moral. Bd. VII. S. 324.
278. Also sprach Zarathustra. Bd. VI. S. 205.
279. Ibid.
280. Der Wille zur Macht, § 71, 475. Bd. XV. S. 70, 481.
281. Ibid., § 72. S. 71.
282. Ibid., § 388. S. 415.
283. Der Wille zur Macht, § 386. Bd. XV. S. 414.
284. Ibid., § 390. S. 420–421.
285. Ibid., § 389. S. 418–419.
286. Ibid., § 409. S. 434.
287. Ibid., § 404. S. 431.
288. Die fröhliche Wissenschaft, § 354. Bd. V. S. 290–294.
289. Götzendämmerung. Bd. VIII. S. 2.
290. Also sprach Zarathustra. Bd. VI. S. 87.
291. Nachträge zum Zarathustra, § 673–674. Bd. XII. S. 357–358
292. Also sprach Zarathustra. Bd. VI. S. 19.
293. Ibid. S. 296; Der Wille zur Macht, § 480. Bd. XV. S. 485–486.
294. Nachträge zum Zarathustra, § 682. Bd. XII. S. 361.
295. Also sprach Zarathustra. Bd. VI. S. 13.
296. Ibid. S. 16.
297. Also sprach Zarathustra. Bd. VI. S. 13.
298. Ibid. S. 16, 418.
299. Ibid. S. 411, 123.
300. Ibid. S. 418, 16.
301. Ibid. S. 16, 419.
302. Ibid. S. 288.
303. Ibid. S. 206; Nachträge zum Zarathustra, § 677. Bd. XII. S. 360.
304. Nachträge zum Zarathustra, § 685. Bd. XII. S. 361.
305. Ibid., § 680. S. 360.
306. Also sprach Zarathustra. Bd. VI. S. 291.
307. Ibid. S. 177, 236, 424; Nachträge zum Zarathustra, § 687. Bd. XII. S. 362.
308. Nachträge zum Zarathustra, § 692. Bd. XII. S. 362.

309. Also sprach Zarathustra. Bd. VI. S. 206.
310. Also sprach Zarathustra. Bd. VI. S. 14.
311. Nachträge zum Zarathustra, § 676. Bd. XII. S. 359.
312. Die fröhliche Wissenschaft, § 15. Bd. V. S. 54–55.
313. Zur Genealogie der Moral. Bd. VII. S. 337.
314. Götzendämmerung. Bd. VIII. S. 145–148.
315. Der Wille zur Macht, § 16. Bd. XV. S. 32.
316. Nachträge zum Zarathustra, § 675. Bd. XII. S. 358.
317. Also sprach Zarathustra. Bd. VI. S. 206.
318. Also sprach Zarathustra. Bd. VI. S. 188; cf. generally S. 186–196; Menschliches, Allzumenschliches, § 164. Bd. II. S. 171–174.
319. Jenseits von Gut und Böse, § 97. Bd. VII. S. 98.
320. Aus der Zeit des Zarathustra, § 68. Bd. VIII. S. 250.
321. Also sprach Zarathustra. Bd. VI. S. 187, 115.
322. Cf. above, § X; see also the previously cited saying about the "true teacher" Jenseits von Gut und Böse, § 63. Bd. VII. S. 92.
323. Also sprach Zarathustra. Bd. VI. S. 28.
324. Nachträge zum Zarathustra, § 706. Bd. XII. S. 365.
325. Nachträge zum Zarathustra, § 707. Bd. XII. S. 365.
326. Ibid., § 705.
327. Ibid., § 707.
328. Also sprach Zarathustra. Bd. VI. S. 399.
329. Ibid. S. 428.
330. Ibid. S. 57–58.
331. Ibid. S. 159.
332. Götzendämmerung. Bd. VIII. S. 165.
333. Der Wille zur Macht, § 62. Bd. VIII. S. 314.
334. Also sprach Zarathustra. Bd. VI. S. 29.
335. Brandes. Menschen und Werke. S. 223.
336. Der Fall Wagner. Bd. VIII. S. 1.

www.ingramcontent.com/pod-product-compliance
Lightning Source LLC
Chambersburg PA
CBHW050251010526
44107CB00003B/274